Greater China and U.S. Foreign Policy

GREATER CHINA
AND
U.S. FOREIGN POLICY

The Choice between Confrontation and Mutual Respect

edited by

Thomas A. Metzger

and

Ramon H. Myers

HOOVER INSTITUTION PRESS
STANFORD UNIVERSITY, STANFORD, CALIFORNIA

Hoover Press Publication No. 433

First printing, 1996
01 00 99 98 97   9 8 7 6 5 4 3 2

Manufactured in the United States of America
The paper used in this publication meets the minimum requirements of American National Standard for Information Sciences—Permanence of Paper for Printed Library Materials, ANSI Z39.48-1984. ⊗

Library of Congress Cataloging-in-Publication Data

    Greater China and U.S. foreign policy : the choice between confrontation and mutual respect / edited by Thomas A. Metzger and Ramon H. Myers.
        p.   cm.
    Includes bibliographical references and index.
    ISBN 0-8179-9412-2
    1. United States—Foreign relations—China. 2. China—foreign relations—United States. 3. China—Politics and government—1976– 4. Chinese reunification question, 1949– I. Metzger, Thomas A., 1933– . II. Myers, Ramon Hawley, 1929– .
E183.8.C5G723   1996
327.73051—dc20   95–48242
                                                CIP

CONTENTS

PREFACE

On December 6–7, 1994, the Hoover Institution hosted a conference on "U.S. Foreign Policy and Greater China." Shortly afterward, and rather surprisingly, Sino-U.S. relations drastically deteriorated. Today, neither country has an ambassador in the other. China has just expelled two U.S. Air Force officers on charges of spying. It has arrested U.S. citizen and human rights activist Harry Wu on charges of espionage (he was subsequently tried, sentenced to fifteen years in jail, and expelled from China). When U.S. secretary of state Warren Christopher met his Chinese counterpart in Brunei in early August 1995, they failed to resolve the crisis. As Henry Kissinger put it around this time, Sino-American relations are in a state of "free fall."

Meanwhile, some pundits have been urging the United States to "contain" China. According to *The Economist*, containing China "should not mean ringing China with nuclear weapons, as the West did the Soviet Union." Instead, Western and Asian countries should work together to persuade China not to use force to settle its grievances. At the same time, Western countries should form a united front in dealing with China and "gradually . . . expand ties with Taiwan" (July 31, 1995, pp. 11–12). Others, like Charles Krauthammer in *Time* (July 31, 1995, p. 72), have argued that "undermining its pseudo-Marxist but still ruthless dictatorship" should be a goal of U.S. policy toward China and that the United States should intensify the struggle "in the public arena" to realize respect for human rights in China.

What has happened since our December conference, therefore, is precisely the sort of confrontation that my coeditor and I warned against. We believe that this warning is still valid and that the evidence supporting it is effectively gathered in this book.

U.S. foreign policy toward greater China, we believe, should be designed by taking note of the new tendencies transforming that part of the world and then figuring out how, in this new context, U.S. goals can best be pursued. Among these new, post–cold war tendencies, nothing is more important than the seeming unwillingness of the U.S. public to bear the burden of a strong foreign policy projecting U.S. power abroad and so realizing that U.S. "international primacy" which Samuel P. Huntington called for in 1993.[1] With a U.S. public unwilling resolutely to bear this burden, "containment" can be no more than talking loudly while carrying a small stick. On the other hand, given some hopeful tendencies today alive in China, there is a significant chance that a U.S. policy treating China in a businesslike but respectful way as the major power it is rapidly becoming could be successful, encouraging China's leaders to follow the international norms emphasized by the United States and its allies. What the coeditors recommend is not appeasement but a policy respecting the Beijing regime, with all its faults, as a currently irreplaceable structure on the stability and progress of which depend the well-being of more than one billion persons.

Good relations between Washington and Beijing are also fundamental to the security of Taiwan, because the only alternative security arrangement for Taiwan—a defense treaty with the United States—is unavailable. Good relations between Beijing and Washington, however, are impossible if Washington and Taipei together bluntly challenge the parameters that Beijing has imposed on the delicate situation in the Taiwan Strait. No matter how rational and moral Taipei's quest for international respect is, and no matter how outrageous is Beijing's claim that Taiwan is no more than a "rebellious province," both Taipei and Washington should base foreign policy on realistic considerations.

Realistically speaking, the United States today is not ready to define itself as the leader of the free world, to guarantee Taiwan's security, and to project the power needed successfully to contain China. What it can do is build up good relations with Beijing, thus encourage Beijing to deal peacefully with the question of unification, and so give moderate leaders in all three capitals a chance to find compromise solutions for difficult problems.

Such solutions will not be found, however, if extremists in all three capitals take over foreign policy — naive U.S. congresspersons and misinformed pundits demanding that China's domestic structure be promptly restructured to accord with American ideals, demagogues in Taiwan assuring a credulous public that Taiwan can become an independent republic without arousing Beijing's anger, and obtusely nationalistic Beijing hardliners regarding the United States as a hostile, imperialistic power rather than part of a capitalistic, multipolar world system joining which can benefit China.

When the Hoover conference was held last December, no one there supposed that these three kinds of extremists would so soon manage to influence so strongly the foreign policies of their respective governments. We thought our volume would just support diplomatic tendencies that already were under way. Instead, we have to hope it will prove useful for those journalists, academics, and politicians interested in further defusing a crisis that should never have been allowed to arise in the first place. Should this crisis, against all expectations, become reinflamed, both China and the United States would have to ponder a range of highly unpleasant possibilities. As Samuel P. Huntington likes to remind us, history is "messy" and full of unpleasant surprises.

The coeditors wish to thank the director of the Hoover Institution, John Raisian, for sponsoring the conference on which this volume is based. We also thank the Sun Yat-sen Endowment Fund, which made possible this volume's publication. Finally, we are grateful for the assistance given by the Taiwan Economic and Cultural Office in San Francisco, which helped make our conference a success.

Ramon H. Myers
September 1995

INTRODUCTION

The Choice between Confrontation and Mutual Respect

THOMAS A. METZGER AND RAMON H. MYERS

A New Era in U.S. Foreign Policy

L
ike the global climate, the international environment of every society is never static, an ever-changing mix of circumstances that in turn deeply affects the most basic domestic activities. In recent years, for perhaps the third time in its history, the United States has experienced a systemic change in its international environment.[1]

Originally, geography blessed our nation with an ability to isolate itself from much of the international turmoil. The modern technology of transportation and communication, however, gradually turned the world into a "global village." Such was the first transformation.

During the first part of the twentieth century, the United States could face the international turmoil to a large extent by relying on the global structure provided by the British Empire. During World War II, the Allies imagined a revised version of that structure, one based on cooperation between "the Big Four": the United States, Great Britain, the USSR, and China. This dream, however, quickly faded away after the war, when the British Empire collapsed, China was convulsed by a revolution, and relations between the two other members of "the Big Four" turned into the cold war. Such was the second transformation.

Americans then became accustomed to dividing the international world into three camps: the free world, communist adversaries, and the Third World. As Ambassador Richard H. Solomon noted, the United States for two decades pursued a "policy of containment," followed by "two decades of coalition politics."[2] The recent, astounding end of the cold war, leaving the United States as the only superpower, struck some as signifying "the end of history." Yet it actually signified the third systemic transformation of the United States' international environment, rendering invalid "the simple verities that underlay policy during the Cold War period," to quote Solomon again. A new foreign policy era, filled with a new variety of complex dangers and opportunities, will once again test the intellectual, moral, and political mettle of our nation.

It has become fashionable today to dwell on U.S. "mistakes" made during the cold war era. Yet it can be argued, to quote Solomon yet again, that "America's post–World War II China policy, despite the tremendous cost, particularly of the Vietnam War, will in the fullness of history be seen to have been dramatically successful" as a way of containing and eventually "undermining" the USSR. Nevertheless, whatever the extent of our success, few will deny that, during the cold war era, U.S. foreign policy could have been more successful.

Trying today, then, to be more successful than in the past, Americans must wonder whether this time around they will prove better able to fathom the mysteries of global history. Although people often discuss alternative answers to foreign policy questions, the very nature of the foreign policy agenda we should address today is far from obvious. The key to a policy debate may be the way in which issues are formulated, the decisions determining which questions to debate.

Greater China as a U.S. Foreign Policy Problem

Trying to make sense out of this new era of international mysteries by dividing it up, however unsatisfactorily, into problem clusters, one can identify one such cluster as "greater China," that part of the world consisting of the People's Republic of China (PRC) and all the other societies that are not only linguistically and culturally Chinese but also adjacent to the PRC (unlike Singapore). On December 6 and 7, 1994, the Hoover Institution held a conference on how U.S. foreign policy should deal with greater China, assembling a group of experts representing a broad variety of foreign as well as U.S. standpoints. After the conference, Solomon decided against publishing his remarks as a separate paper, but each of the other participants presented a paper based on her or his conference remarks, in some cases elaborating on the latter.

This book is made up of these ten papers. In chapter 1, Ambassador James R. Lilley analyzes the evolution of PRC foreign policy in recent years, especially toward Taiwan and Hong Kong. In chapter 2, Ramon H. Myers looks into the impasse between the PRC and the Republic of China on Taiwan (ROC).[3] In chapters 3 and 4, David M. Lampton and Nicholas R. Lardy respectively examine the security and economic issues facing the United States in its relation with the PRC. In chapters 5 and 6, Merle Goldman and Thomas A. Metzger present two partly different perspectives on human rights in China as a problem for U.S. policy. Chapter 7 is drawn from the conference's concluding roundtable. Each of the four papers in it expresses one of the major political or diplomatic visions that will affect the future of greater China: Guo Changlin's statement is close to official PRC thinking; Lung-chu Chen's expresses a prominent Taiwanese feeling that Taiwan today is a sovereign nation not receiving the international respect it deserves; Hungdah Chiu's illustrates the kind of diplomatic reasoning now often pursued in Taiwan in order to obtain that respect; and Charles Hill's sets forth an American vision of the kind of overarching international framework into which greater China should fit.

It is true that some important matters were barely touched on,

notably the imminent assertion of PRC sovereignty over Hong Kong
and the grave problem of human rights created by PRC policy in Tibet.
Nevertheless, the papers included here cumulatively make clear the
nature of the basic new realities faced by the United States in its deal-
ings with greater China, the questions raised by these new realities, and
the range of disagreement regarding each question.

There was little if any disagreement about what the basic new realities are and the need to raise two questions. First, should the key question be whether to pose a clear-cut choice between confrontation and
mutual respect in U.S.-PRC relations? Second, if so, which option is
more reasonable?

Trying to weave together the insights of the conference participants, the two writers of this introduction argue that the United States
should make a clear-cut choice in favor of mutual accommodation and
respect. We cannot claim, however, that all the participants would agree
with every aspect of our thesis. Each article stands on its own, and none
of these scholars is responsible for anything in this book outside her or
his own statement.

Greater China as a Mix of Four New Realities

One major new reality in east Asia was created when, after Mao Tse-
tung's death in 1976, the PRC gradually changed from a combination
of totalitarianism and socialism to one of authoritarianism and a
"socialist market economy." To be sure, this remarkable transformation, as unpredicted as the end of the cold war, has a dark side.
Lampton's article notes the shadows cast on economic modernization
by an ailing public sector, inflation, unemployment, and the shortage of
energy. Bureaucratic corruption is certainly a problem, although it is
more an object of public outrage than a tendency seriously impeding
economic growth. The problem of economic inequality and relative
deprivation is much more serious, especially in the context of a culture
traditionally lacking any fatalistic belief in caste differences, deeply
valuing the principle of economic equality, and euphorically assuming
that the realization of such equality (*chün-fu*) is well within the practi-

cal ability of any decent government, developing or modernized. Many millions of Chinese are now entering the middle class, but, as Solomon pointed out, that middle class "will be a minuscule portion of the population." Thus a population roughly as big as that of the United States is obtaining significant purchasing power and contributing mightily to the flow of international commerce, but some 800 to 900 million Chinese will remain pitifully impoverished and seriously frustrated for the foreseeable future.

Apart from this question of inequality and other economic difficulties, there is the question of the extent to which the PRC will be able to "control the resources that could be aggregated" by the high rate of economic growth that is likely to continue, as Solomon put it. During the Ming-Ch'ing period (1368–1912), the Chinese empire became increasingly unable to mobilize resources. It turned into an "inhibited political center" the moral legitimization of which in the eyes of its subjects was only partial, which sought to head off political unrest by giving leeway to a large private economic sector and keeping tax rates exceedingly low, and which greatly and confusedly decentralized the management of what taxes it did collect.[4] There is considerable evidence that the PRC leadership today, trying to cope with the multiplex and increasingly articulated desires of such a huge population more inclined to tolerate than patriotically support it, will be forced by the sheer inertia of its situation to revert back to this traditional mode of "the inhibited political center."[5] For good or for ill, its inability to mobilize resources may well limit its international role.

Another result could be an enduring, potentially dangerous sense of political insecurity and inferiority. The "inhibited center" has long been a fact of Chinese institutional history, not a condition Chinese elites legitimized. In imperial times, they vigorously criticized their inhibited center as part of a degenerate world contradicting the Confucian ideal of a morally unified society. Then, ever since the turn of the century, when the Chinese began to perceive their society as "backward" compared to "Europe and America" (*Ou-Mei*), their ideological mainstream focused on the hope of fully mobilizing their society's energies and so "surpassing Europe and America." Today this hope has turned into the widespread belief that "the twenty-first century will be a Chinese century." In the light of this tradition-rooted belief in the moral unity and international centrality of China, weak Chinese political integration will undoubtedly distress politically articulate Chinese circles.

Moreover, this increasing disaggregation of social and political impulses, the mix of inflation and other economic difficulties, and the rising sense of relative deprivation have to be put into the context of that continuation of human rights violations in the PRC described in Goldman's article as well as that of the current democracy movement she analyzed in a recent book.[6] Metzger's article argues that such violations to some extent are unavoidable, given the very nature of a non-democratic regime the stability of which partly depends on limiting the scope of political dissent, and which, in the eyes of many observers, cannot practicably carry out prompt democratization. Nevertheless, these violations fuel the passions of an oppositional movement that could become formidable, even though it currently remains weak and largely scattered overseas, much as did the revolutionary movement during the last decade of the last dynasty, which fell in 1912. As Hill notes, "the Chinese revolution, which has been going on for at least a century and a half, is not over yet."

Nevertheless, despite all such doubts about the future of the PRC, many observers have been struck by the PRC's great economic capabilities and its stellar record of economic growth, discussed in both Lardy's article and Lampton's; by the contrast between the successes of the Chinese in dealing with their socialist heritage and the failures of the Russians in dealing with theirs;[7] and by the resolute, ingenious policies with which the PRC bureaucracy today is trying to deal with the ills of its public sector, accommodating a great variety of local economic impulses in a way that is quite familiar to students of Ming-Ch'ing history.[8]

No one at the conference subscribed to the fashionable notion that the PRC has become a "paralyzed" state unable effectively to pursue economic modernization, that, given its economic backwardness and problems in political organization, the PRC can be dismissed by the United States as a minor player on the world stage. Hill notes its "rise to world power." Lampton speaks of "its emergence as a global power," its "emergence as a great power," and its gradually increasing ability to project military strength. Lardy notes "China's emergence as a major world economic power." He explains that in 1993, its exports accounted for 2.5 percent of world exports, it absorbed a third of all "foreign direct investment flowing to developing countries," and it was "the tenth largest U.S. export market." Moreover, he adds, "since 1990 China has been far and away the fastest growing foreign market for U.S. goods"; in the next five years, it is likely to import US $1 trillion in capital goods from the United States and other countries.

Moreover, if history repeats itself, it never does so except partially. Fiscal and political decentralization seem once again to have become a serious problem for China. Yet entirely new possibilities were suggested when Solomon pointed out that China might address its energy shortage problem by building an oil pipeline stretching from Kazakhstan to China's southeast coast, and, not incidentally, enhancing the central government's control over those rambunctious provinces.

While the transformed character of the PRC is one of the new realities confronting U.S. policy in east Asia, so is that of the ROC. Taiwan's "economic miracle," by now one of the most famous success stories of the twentieth century, turned that society into a fully urbanized one, where unemployment hovers around 2 percent, where typical rural folk fly off for their vacations to see the Grand Canyon, where the vast majority of the population see themselves as middle class, and where exports have yielded a foreign reserve (more than US $90 billion) that on many days is the largest in the world. With less than 2 percent of the PRC's population, Taiwan today has a gross national product equal to perhaps 30 percent of the PRC's and is the United States' sixth or seventh largest trading partner. Myers's article describes how economic modernization was followed by democratization. Taiwan is an almost unique member of what Samuel P. Huntington calls "the third wave" of democratization in world history, in that the ruling party there during the authoritarian era, the Kuomintang, was not repudiated when free elections began.[9] Myers also discusses how democratization there has become intertwined with the rise of Taiwanese nationalism, an increasingly widespread feeling that Taiwan must remain economically and politically distinct from the mainland. Yet, as Solomon notes, there has not yet been any "headlong rush in support of independence." This point is illustrated by Chen's article. The spirit of Taiwanese nationalism is evident in Chen's statement that "Taiwan is a sovereign, independent state in every sense of the word," while prudence is evident in his judgment that there "is no need for Taiwan to declare independence now."

While the character of the ROC as well as that of the PRC has been transformed, a third new reality is the transformed character of relations between the two. Certainly this transformation reflects the new international statures of the two: the PRC's emerging status as a world power and the increasing international respect enjoyed by Taiwan as a democratic society with a great economic impact on not only greater China but also the United States and many other parts of the world. This change in the international statures of the two has been complemented by a fundamental shift in their relations away from hostile confrontation and toward peace and increasing economic traffic, if not increasing economic interdependence. As Lampton argues, such interdependence implies a bias toward peace in that "economic interpenetration raises the potential costs of conflict for all involved parties and leads to the creation of constituencies in each society that will promote stability and seek to avoid catastrophic conflict." Cultural exchanges and many personal visits have strengthened this bias, which also was strengthened in July 1994, when, as Myers notes, "the ROC . . . acknowledged the sovereign existence of the PRC as a political entity possessing legal authority over the Chinese mainland."

To be sure, this bias toward peace is still under the shadow of the continuing impasse between the PRC and the ROC, analyzed by Myers. The PRC did not reciprocate the ROC's 1994 acknowledgment. Their impasse is nicely illustrated by the way that both Chen and Guo reject even the term "greater China" as a category with which to define the subject matter of our conference. Guo, his view coinciding with the official PRC position, states that "what experts refer to as 'Greater China' today is actually China as it should be." Speaking for many in Taiwan though not for the ROC government, Chen contradicts him: "Taiwan is Taiwan, and China is China. . . . Taiwan is not part of 'Greater China,' not to mention China."

Moreover, as both Myers and Chiu point out, this impasse has become a potentially dangerous vicious circle: the PRC, trying to prevent the ROC from playing an independent international role, works continuously to isolate the ROC internationally; this process of isolation insults the Taiwanese and fans the flames of Taiwanese nationalism; to curry favor with angry Taiwanese voters, the Kuomintang-led government develops an ambitious foreign policy seeking to upgrade its international status; the PRC reacts to these ROC demands by trying further to isolate it. In other words, the PRC policy of isolation pours oil instead of water on the flames of Taiwanese nationalism and so makes it increasingly difficult for ROC president Lee Teng-hui to persuade Taiwan's voters to support his one-China policy. Should they end up not supporting it, the PRC would find itself having to choose between two options neither of which it can welcome: abandoning the goal of unification or creating a major, if not bloody, international crisis by trying to force unification on the people of Taiwan.

So far, however, both sides have prudently emphasized the correlated goals of peace and mutually beneficial economic traffic. This point is illustrated also by Lilley's analysis of how in recent years the PRC has dealt with the impasse in the Taiwan Straits. His interpretation implies, just as Guo's statement shows, that the PRC remains extremely reluctant to deal with this impasse in any but a peaceful way.

As Lilley explains, before its slaughter of students on June 4, 1989, turned much world opinion against it, the PRC pursued a policy of increasing economic integration between itself, the ROC, and Hong Kong, hoping that economic integration would facilitate political absorption. After that date, this policy suffered a series of setbacks, not only in Taiwan and Hong Kong but also in terms of a variety of domestic, foreign policy, and military problems, including the cold shock of Desert Storm, which forced PRC leaders to realize how backward their military technology was.

Reacting to these setbacks, they certainly were animated by their nationalistic determination to turn China into a great world power, as Lampton suggests. Yet any such nationalism did not lead them seriously to consider the use of force in dealing with Taiwan. As Lilley sees it, "In Chinese foreign policy, there has often been a struggle between the so-called nationalistic, anti-imperialistic, anticolonial line and the pragmatic international line." Lilley offers much evidence to show that the latter is currently on the upswing. He notes that China currently is emphasizing Western and Japanese inputs as indispensable for its modernization programs. In the context of the South China Sea islands and their petroleum potential, its relations with the Association of Southeast Asian Nations (ASEAN), and its border problems with Vietnam, China has come to deemphasize military intentions and look for legal solutions. It sided with the United States against Saddam Hussein in Desert Storm, and it has begun "to use its influence and leverage on North Korea to seek a denuclearization of the peninsula as well as economic reform of North Korea." Moreover, Lilley points out, it "has joined the Missile Technology Control Regime, the Nuclear Nonproliferation Treaty, and the Berne Convention on intellectual property rights, and it has participated actively in international antidrug campaigns."

To be sure, Lilley's optimism in this regard is not universally shared. There are complaints about the PRC's international behavior, such as the claim that it recently occupied an atoll in the Spratly Islands violating the Law of the Sea Convention it signed in 1982. Mark J. Valencia of the East-West Center recently analyzed the multinational tensions converging on this chain of atolls.[10] Moreover, as Lilley notes, the PRC is emphasizing a "selective military buildup" with which eventually to intimidate Taiwan. Another problem was noted by Solomon. Given both its need for Middle East oil and its legitimate security concerns regarding its own Muslim population, the PRC has come into conflict with U.S. policy by trying to cultivate its relations with some Middle Eastern states, recently carrying out military and nuclear technology sales to Iran or planning them. Similarly, a March 1995 Heritage Foundation *Backgrounder* says, "While promising to adhere to terms of the Missile Technology and Control Regime in 1992, Beijing is suspected of transferring M-9 intermediate range ballistic missile technology to Pakistan."[11] Hill says that "China . . . as it grows in wealth and power, seems increasingly ready to overlook, ignore, or push aside" the international principles traditionally defended by the United States and the West (see below) "or to employ them when to do so would benefit the PRC's interest and not to employ them when another might benefit."

Lilley's judgment, however, is more hopeful: "China obviously acts in its own interests but in case after case, its interests are becoming closer to prevailing international views. . . . In other words, the Chinese are integrating their system with the world system." Goldman has a similar view: "China in the Deng era is concerned with its image in the world and wants to be accepted as a member of the establishment." Lilley adds, "There may, therefore, be emerging a more flexible faction within the Chinese communist leadership. Characteristics of this faction could be rule of law under the auspices of [the National Party Congress] led by Qiao Shi with a focus on economic issues." In other words, the internal transformation of the PRC seems to have some connection to a "pragmatic international line" in foreign policy, and this line includes an emphasis on peace and increasing economic traffic in the Taiwan Straits.

While relations between the PRC and the ROC have thus been transformed along with the internal transformations of these two societies, these three new realities in east Asia clearly entail some causal connections, however hard to specify, with a fourth reality, changes in the broader, global arena. The end of the cold war of course transformed relations between the four major powers in the western Pacific (the United States, the PRC, Japan, and Russia). The threat of a major war has receded, and PRC-U.S. relations are no longer based on a shared need to check any Soviet expansionism. Moreover, as Hill notes, "this now is a world in which the United States shows no inclination to play the role of constructive balancer and intervener that it held during the cold war." Some may feel that the United States is mistakenly responding to the end of the cold war just as it did to the end of World War II by prematurely assuming that this costly victory has produced a satisfactory world order no longer dependent on U.S. exertions abroad. It is almost a law of history, after all, that imperialism or the projection of power abroad is often unpopular with not only the populations subject to it but also the citizens asked to bear the burden of a strong foreign policy. This burden has been especially unpopular with U.S. voters still clinging to the illusion of a return to that tranquil state of geographical isolation enjoyed by their ancestors before the modern era. Whether or not this new American turn inward is mistaken, however, it is part of the new global reality. So is a shift in the distribution of economic power from West to East, complicated in turn, as Lampton notes, by the rising economic importance of "developing" nations in comparison with that of "rich industrial countries."

Thus while the relative economic importance of greater China in the global context is increasing, the United States' turn inward means that stability in east Asia increasingly depends on the leadership of the PRC. By definition, a multipolar world lacks the guaranteed stability provided by a central, dominant power. Not enjoying geographical isolation, unable to rely on a friendly empire, and unwilling to bear the burden of a pax Americana, the United States today, in east Asia as elsewhere, has no choice but to deal with the uncertainties of a multipolar world.

Issues and Recommendations

If, then, as the conference essentially agreed, greater China today is largely shaped by four new realities (the transformed nature of the PRC, that of the ROC, the shift toward peace in relations between the PRC and ROC, and the end of the cold war), what problems and opportunities do these new realities pose for U.S. foreign policy?

Because the United States has traditionally combined and will continue to combine realpolitik with a quest for morality in foreign policy, human rights abuses in a nondemocratic country like the PRC constitute a serious foreign policy issue for the United States.

On the economic front, as discussed by Lardy, a major problem is the large deficit suffered by the United States in its trade with the PRC. Lardy notes that it is smaller than it appears. He explains one should take into account much bilateral trade with China that passes through Hong Kong and is counted as U.S.–Hong Kong trade; value added to Chinese exports in Hong Kong as they pass through there on their way to the United States; and the way that the rising U.S. deficit with the PRC is partly balanced by declining deficits with Hong Kong and the ROC (given that many businesses previously exporting to the United States from locations in Taiwan and Hong Kong have now shifted their operations to the PRC).

Yet even with these adjustments, the U.S. deficit with the PRC is large. It is partly caused by the PRC's gross violations of intellectual property rights, a continuing problem despite a February 1995 agreement signed by the PRC,[12] as well as by a variety of access problems discussed by Lardy. These latter problems in turn cloud the PRC's attempt to join the General Agreement on Tariffs and Trade / World Trade Organization (GATT/WTO). Because of the great success of the PRC as an exporter, the United States is reluctant to give it the "special and differential treatment" enjoyed by WTO members whose economies are regarded as "developing." Moreover, Lardy adds, there have been Chinese violations of the Multifiber Agreement limiting certain kinds of exports to the United States; complaints around the world that certain PRC enterprises have not met their credit obligations; and charges that some of the PRC exports are goods produced by prison labor.

The security problems, discussed especially by Lilley and Lampton, are at least as serious. More precisely, there are four sets of dormant or probably manageable problems, and two sets that pose no present danger but could eventually generate serious crises.

One currently dormant problem that nevertheless has been central to Asian history is the long border between the PRC and Russia.[13] Second, there are policy clashes between the United States and the PRC with regard to Iran and Pakistan, relations with whom the PRC tries to cultivate at least partly to keep its own Muslim populations docile and to secure its oil sources. Third, there is the impasse with Taiwan. Fourth, there is the range of other east Asian problems touched on by Lilley: relations between ASEAN and the PRC, the border with Vietnam, conflicting claims in the South China Sea, the dormant problem of the Tiaoyutai Islands (Senkaku), and PRC influence on North Korea.

The truly central security problems are those posed by the PRC's potential military strength and the possibility of the PRC's economic deterioration and political instability. Lilley notes the emphasis of PRC leaders on military modernization, partly as a way of keeping the military establishment content; Lampton speaks of the PRC's "gradually expanding military strength"; and Hill warns that "the powers of Asia could well become the focus of a new pattern of nuclear arms buildup." Lampton, however, in thinking about "greater China security issues," puts his emphasis on the undesirable effects of serious economic and political deterioration in the PRC: "Among them would be accelerated migration, a more assertive and nationalistic foreign policy, an inability of China's political center to control the behavior of local authorities . . . and there would be a staggering human toll."

In other words, the United States, paradoxically enough, is faced by a potential economic-military rival in the well-being and success of which it has a material as well as a moral interest. How should the United States handle its disagreements with such a power?

There was little if any disagreement in the conference that the best way to handle them was to integrate China further into what Lilley calls "the world system." As Lampton puts it, "America must seize the window of opportunity provided by the next decade of China's rise to work with Beijing to assure that China is productively and appropriately involved in regional and global economic and security structures." Hill develops the idea of "the modern international system of cooperation" as a normative order which has, with interruptions, been emerging during the last three centuries, which all nations today, the United States as well as China, should respect more, and which is based on six, partly overlapping, still evolving principles or kinds of institutions: the sovereign rights of states, international law, international organizations, an emphasis on open trade, human rights, and systems of international security.

Building a bit on Hill's concept, one can note that, while much current Western political theory has focused on the deficiencies of capitalism, nationalism, and Millsian democracy (what John Dunn calls "the modern constitutional representative democratic republic"), many today agree that Millsian democracy is the only known practicable way to approximate the goal of government by "the people," that capitalism is the only effective way to bring about modern economic growth, and that the nation-state is an indispensable kind of human grouping. From this standpoint, one can envisage a normative world system made up of modern societies each combining these three features and linking up with the others by respecting the six kinds of principles or institutions Hill emphasizes.

Yet pursuit of this ideal has to be combined with some notion about the appropriate way to deal with our actual, contemporary international community, many members of which are not modern societies in the above sense. In such an imperfect world filled with many unmodern societies, to what extent does one need to accommodate political patterns that seem morally unsatisfactory or irrational, such as nondemocratic governments or the demands of major powers for deference, in order to pursue goals like peace, stability, and economic development?

Thinkers like Sun Yat-sen have viewed such an imperfect world as a transitional historical "stage" and have emphasized adapting political norms to suit the needs of different stages. Similarly, John Stuart Mill believed that democracy ("liberty") was appropriate only for "civilized" societies. In contemporary American circles, however, such "stage" theories of history have been widely rejected, and so has been the logically linked idea of flexibly adapting human rights to the developmental needs of unmodern societies. Nevertheless, many today recognize that an unmodern society like the PRC cannot quickly democratize, and that the need for stability in a nondemocratic context regrettably implies forcibly stopping destabilizing movements calling for prompt democratization (see Metzger article).

Indeed, the problem of how to apply human rights to a nondemocratic, unmodern, culturally exotic society is a deep one that cannot be solved through the procrustean application of uniform standards of morality and rationality. On the other hand, we who believe in such standards should vigorously participate in the global discussion of them, trying gradually to persuade everyone to respect them.

For instance, in depicting a normative international order as a historical process evolving over the centuries, Hill is pointing to a kind of development which Chinese in modern times of all ideological persuasions have often perceived as "an irresistible tide in the flow of global history" (*shih-chieh-te ch'ao-liu*), a trend conformity with which is the key to national success. The teleological notion of such historical "tides" is highly controversial in the West but virtually unchallenged in Chinese discussions. If the building up of a modern international system can be cogently and repeatedly presented to the Chinese as such an "irresistible tide in world history," the Chinese may increasingly come to accept this "system." Moreover, the idea of such a world system has a distinctive affinity with the culturally deep-rooted tendency of the

Chinese to envisage a world order harmoniously based on universal moral principles (*ta-t'ung*) rather than one unpredictably dependent on the ebb and flow of clashing civilizations. Since academic U.S. historians study international relations only in an empirical way, a State Department scholar could usefully prepare a documented historical study showing how the modern international system has gradually evolved and explaining how its further evolution would serve China's national self-interest and converge with traditionally central Chinese ideals. Institutionalizing such a world system entails vigorously propagating its raison d'etre in terms which Chinese can agree make sense.

Ideally, such a modern international system in any part of the world should rest on multilateral agreements between the most powerful nations in that area. In this case, as Hill and Lampton note, there should be increasing cooperation between China, the United States, Japan, and Russia. Such cooperation could facilitate linkages between issues. For instance, if China's border problems with Russia were resolved, it might feel more comfortable about compromising on Taiwan. At present, such multilateral cooperation is impeded by a variety of factors, such as Moscow's current inability to control regional authorities in the Russian far east and to effect a unified foreign policy.[14] Nevertheless, the United States should still try imaginatively to develop multilateral relations in east Asia.

Whether or not multilateral relations can be developed, a "complex game of balance of power politics . . . is likely to emerge in East Asia," as Solomon said. To be sure, as Hill suggests, any such game should be put into the context of a shared international commitment to the "modern international system of cooperation." As just mentioned, however, we live in an imperfect world. Thus the United States has to make a key decision on the extent to which U.S. power should be projected in this part of the world.

There is little doubt that this decision will be based on neither Samuel P. Huntington's call for a pax Americana nor isolationism. Searching for some middle ground, many Americans will agree with Lampton's point that "a continued, significant American forward military presence in East Asia will be an indispensable element, if stability is to be maintained."

Valid as this point is, however, it does not fully address the problem of how basically to structure the U.S.-PRC relation. To be sure, since, as Lampton notes, "China is unwilling to concede that American military forces in the region are a stabilizing influence," the two sides can stabilize their relation by trying to resolve their disagreement about such military or diplomatic issues. Yet resolution of this disagreement as well as the others will depend on how the two states design their general, overarching way of dealing with each other.

Certainly the United States should design a relationship which includes a firm U.S. commitment to its basic principles and interests, as illustrated by the U.S.-PRC negotiations in February 1995 moving toward the protection of intellectual property rights. Many feel that PRC leaders are shrewd, unscrupulous practitioners of realpolitik who typically posture and bully to get what they want without accommodating the interests of other nations, and that the United States should not let itself be bullied by them. We fully agree.

Within the context of such firmness, however, there is a choice between a confrontational approach and a more accommodative one based on mutual respect. Lampton's approach illustrates what we here call an "accommodative" policy: "In short, Americans should assume that: China will succeed; China will thereby become increasingly important; we should do what we can (with Beijing's cooperation) to smooth China's way to full and equal participation in the global community; and, China's success is to be greatly preferred over its failure." Lardy's specific recommendations regarding the whole range of economic issues, including GATT/WTO, also illustrate what we mean by "accommodative." Moreover, none of the speakers at the conference favored re-linking economic and human rights issues.

We would add that this accommodative approach implies psychological, rhetorical, public acceptance by the United States that China is one of the world's major powers, a proud nation naturally entitled to develop effective military forces, not just a part of "the developing world" graciously encouraged by the United States to carry out economic modernization. For instance, the highest U.S. leaders should formally and regularly meet with the highest PRC leaders. After all, moralistic objections to such meetings are no more valid than were earlier objections to meetings between U.S. and Soviet leaders. Similarly, the United States could try harder to deal with east Asian issues by actively promoting multilateral discussions including the PRC, instead of emphasizing bilateral relations converging on Washington.

The "accommodative" approach implies adult, businesslike, mutually respectful relations between the PRC and the United States, without further American efforts to treat the PRC as a junior partner, not to mention defining it a delinquent requiring rehabilitation. It implies acknowledging a multipolar world in which the PRC is one major power among others. If any major power is entitled to some deference or benefit of the doubt, we cannot reasonably preclude that degree of courtesy when dealing with the PRC. To be sure, such deference has to be combined with the firmness mentioned above. The skill to square this circle is precisely what statesmen are expected to have.

The more confrontational approach is currently popular in some American political and media circles. The Heritage Foundation's *Backgrounder,* no. 243, put out March 29, 1995, "China Should Adhere to Rules of the Road," depicts China as a delinquent nation "defying international norms of behavior" with regard to the whole range of human rights, security, and economic issues outlined above, recommends that the "U.S. must make clear to Beijing that such behavior is unacceptable to the entire international community," and seeks U.S.-PRC discussions restricted to "specific issues," as opposed to becoming "bogged down in theoretical and never-ending discussion of the general U.S.-China relationship." This more confrontational approach, in other words, discounts the psychological, rhetorical aspects of these relations.

As already mentioned, the two authors of the Introduction cannot claim that our Hoover conference produced an unqualified consensus favoring the "accommodative" approach, but they favor it. To be sure, as they have long insisted, perhaps more strongly than many other American scholars, the modernization of China has been immensely impeded by the tragic fact that for three decades the mainland was subjected to the dysfunctions and horrors of the Maoist regime, unable to apply those effective methods of modernization and democratization so brilliantly illustrated by the Taiwan experience, and many of the effects of that tragic era persist today.

Today, however, what Lampton criticizes as "a sanctions-based, punitive approach to the Chinese" would indeed be counterproductive. No one denies, after all, that China today is an emerging world power in both military and economic terms, and that incorporating it into the modern world system of international cooperation has to be the main goal of U.S. China policy, the key step needed to deal successfully with the whole range of human rights, economic, and security issues. But how can such incorporation be best carried out?

As already suggested, if the United States saw itself as the leader of the free, civilized world, ready to impose an international order on recalcitrant nations, a more confrontational approach might make sense. For good or for ill, however, the United States today is not ready to play that role. Therefore, it cannot expect to have a major say about how some one billion people in a distant part of the world will settle their affairs. We cannot talk loudly and carry a small stick. If we want China to participate in the world system, China itself must want to participate, feeling that participation serves its national interests.

Americans like to think of national interests in pragmatic, specific terms, but China's national interests include a distinctive, emotional vision of its own importance, indeed centrality, in world affairs. If U.S. statesmen do not succeed in conveying respect for this Chinese vision, Chinese will be unable to legitimize in their own minds that world system of international cooperation in the construction of which we want them to join. Dealing with specific disagreements between two nations is important, but, to the extent that international relations also depend on personal relationships between leaders and certain more diffuse types of mutual understanding and trust, Americans will have to understand or at least sympathetically respond to that Chinese self-image.

Doing that will be difficult for us. We have easily oscillated between the contempt felt by a Joseph Stilwell for certain Chinese ways, the admiration expressed by a Henry Kissinger for the dynamic leadership abilities displayed by a Mao Tse-tung, and the strangely inextinguishable hope, ingeniously encouraged by the Chinese themselves, that the Chinese Communists are simply pragmatists like us, who publicly insist on retaining their peculiar ideology only to placate some silly but powerless members of their society. What we have not really confronted is China's self-image as a major power in charge of its own destiny, second in dignity to no other nation, and, in some mysterious way, responsible for the moral order of the whole world.[15] This Chinese self-image, a traditional mind-set as deeply rooted as the Jews' belief that they are God's Chosen People (indeed, both beliefs stem from what Karl Jaspers called "the axial age"), cannot but strike Americans as irrational and indeed collides with our own self-image as the world's greatest nation as well as the common view that the West is the world's model civilization. Yet especially in a multicultural, multipolar international arena, statesmen must find ways to deal respectfully even with a nation whose self-image may strike them as irrational, so long as this perceived irrationality does not entail concrete actions unacceptable to them. U.S.-Chinese relations will proceed smoothly only if Americans find a way to respect China's vision of its importance in the world while simultaneously staying true to their own ideals and the principles of the emerging world system. As the one superpower, the United States assumes it is a kind of primus inter pares, even in a multipolar world. Unless it is willing to bear the burden of a strong foreign policy, however, it had better put the emphasis on "pares."

After all, during World War Two, Americans felt comfortable respecting China's stature as one of "the Big Four." To be sure, such respect implies that the respected nation operates at a certain minimum moral level, and the PRC's record on human rights today continues to appall many throughout the world. Nevertheless, the United States today can respect the PRC as a major world power and still regard itself as pursuing a moral foreign policy. As argued in Metzger's chapter, the moral mission of U.S. foreign policy should be to favor modernizing developments that promise practicably to increase the well-being of a people, practicably to promote "the greatest happiness of the greatest number." As indicated above, given an imperfect international community many members of which have not yet realized the modern combination of nationalism, capitalism, and Millsian democracy, enhancing the well-being of a particular society does not necessarily mean opposing all nondemocratic practices. China's further modernization depends above all on the stability of the current regime and its confident participation in the international system, not on the utopian hopes of those dissidents who call for rapid democratization and contemptuously discount their government's pragmatic and gradualistic efforts.

Again, being wary of the utopianism and one-sidedness often coloring the messages coming from Chinese dissident circles does not mean canceling the American concern with human rights. Our point is that morality in foreign policy should be pursued in a practical, prudent, effective way. This includes the methods described in Goldman's article, especially engaging "China on human rights issues in a variety of public forums, particularly in international arenas," continuously confronting China with the prospect of public censure. The United States should take full advantage of the PRC's deep desire to be respected as an exemplary society at the center of the world system of nations.

Moreover, this approach is promising. Deeply desiring to be internationally admired, the PRC, having loosened the controls over its citizens, can no longer depend on its original totalitarian ability to keep its human rights abuses hidden from the global media. Some elites in the PRC are also bound to be sensitive to domestic as well as international pressures. As an "inhibited political center," the PRC will find itself increasingly unable to depend on regimentation and terror, increasingly dependent on the acquiescence of urbanized strata aware of world opinion and valuing not only personal freedom but also predictability in the conduct of public affairs. Full political freedom such as Taiwan now enjoys cannot be quickly realized in the PRC, but the outlook for human rights there is definitely not dark.

Focusing all these domestic and international pressures on the PRC is absolutely integral to the ongoing transformation of the PRC, but the success of this transformation also depends on the stability of the government. There is nothing morally embarrassing about prudently combining a strong interest in human rights with an appreciation of the practical conditions on which the well-being of more than one billion souls depends.

It is this combination which should serve as the moral basis of an "accommodative" U.S. policy toward China. Such a policy, meshing with the "pragmatic international line" in the PRC and facilitating China's participation in the world system, offers hope of resolving the PRC-ROC impasse. A corollary of this accommodative approach is that

China cannot be expected to give up its belief that there is only one China and that Taiwan is part of it, a point also long affirmed by the United States. The need somewhat to accommodate an emerging global power like the PRC is not an entirely pleasant fact, but it must be faced by the people of Taiwan as well as the United States. Given the unwillingness of the United States today to defend Taiwan against an invasion from the mainland, the security of Taiwan depends in significant part on China's desire to participate in the international system, and such participation, as has just been argued, requires respect for the most vital interests of the PRC, including its one-China belief.

Such respect, however, must be complemented by the PRC's recognition of the historical reality of Taiwan as 21 million people who have been extraordinarily successful in both economic and political terms, who cannot be forced to accept a form of governance they do not want, who rightfully seek full membership in the international community, and who have the military capability to inflict significant damage on the PRC should it act aggressively toward them. Respecting the most vital interests of the PRC does not mean agreeing that it rather than the democratic government of Taiwan should decide how Taiwan should be governed. A major power seeking the respect of the world cannot inflexibly adhere to propositions striking the world as at odds with historical reality, such as the idea that Taiwan is just a "renegade province" whose people wish to be part of the PRC. *Chih-lu wei-ma* (pointing to a deer and forcing people to call it a horse) may have worked in the courts of ancient tyrants, but it is certainly not a promising tactic for modern governments wanting to be respected by the international community.

If the United States were to stand by passively while the PRC imposed its will on the people of Taiwan, the United States would not only lose international prestige but also violate its own deepest sense of what is right. Two great powers trying to accommodate each other's most vital national interests and deepest beliefs cannot ask each other to discard these beliefs.

Resolution of the impasse between the ROC and the PRC, therefore, seems contingent on a revision of the relationship between the United States and the PRC: each should give the other the respect to which a great power is entitled. On the one hand, the PRC should not expect the United States to acquiesce in any takeover of Taiwan. On the other, the United States, to the extent it is unwilling to pay the price of a pax Americana, should accept the reality of a multipolar world and so should try to satisfy the PRC leaders' deep need to enjoy the prestige of representing a major world power. If they can enjoy this prestige by playing a leading role in "the world system," they may become more ready to believe that imposing their authority on Taiwan is not urgently needed to realize this prestige. In other words, they may be willing to reach a compromise on Taiwan if such a compromise is seen by them as something generously agreed to by them as prestigious leaders of the world system. At the very least, this is psychologically different from being sternly told to respect the world system as a standard upheld by the West and not yet reached by wayward nations like China.

But even if the United States and the PRC can agree on the character of their overall relation, how can any compromise between the PRC and the ROC be reached? John Dunn has said that "nationalism is the starkest political shame of the twentieth century."[16] Whether or not one entirely agrees with him, it is clear that blindly nationalistic impulses on both sides of the Strait have to be curbed. That should be feasible, however, given the prudence that so far has characterized Taiwanese nationalism as well as the "pragmatic international line" now influential in the PRC. Both sides are well aware that the interests of each are served by the stability and prosperity of the other and by expanding, peaceful economic relations between them.

A compromise would include the PRC's willingness to let Taiwan join various international organizations, as suggested in detail by Chiu's chapter. Certainly it would be helpful if the PRC detached its claim of sovereignty over Taiwan from any right to use force to achieve unification. Extremely useful, however, would be demilitarization of the Taiwan Strait, a de facto renunciation of the use of force, which could eventually entail some withdrawal of ROC military forces from Kinmen and Matsu. In such a peaceful atmosphere, further agreements about navigation and commerce could be reached. The two sides could then deal with the more purely symbolic aspects of their relation, aiming toward a commonwealth arrangement that would preserve not only the one-China ideal but also Taiwan's independence and dignity. Since Taiwan's political independence would be preserved, there would be no need to make establishment of the commonwealth contingent on China's democratization. So far as names go, Taiwan, like Canada, could formally refer to itself by just using its proper name, leaving any-one interested free to decide whether "Taiwan" is a Chinese province or an independent republic.

Conclusion

While an accommodative U.S. policy toward China might thus lead to such a resolution of the impasse between the ROC and the PRC, it is likely that a punitive policy would preclude this outcome. The two authors of this Introduction therefore conclude that, in the post–cold war era as it has unfolded so far, U.S. foreign policy with regard to greater China must deal with four new realities, including the unpleas-ant uncertainties of a multipolar world; in dealing with these realities, the best way for the United States to pursue its human rights, econom-ic, and security objectives is to negotiate with the Chinese on the basis of mutual respect and accommodation; such an approach is more like-ly than a confrontational one to lead to resolution of the dangerous PRC-ROC impasse.

Our recommendation entails much emphasis on the global reality that the end of the cold war left behind: the fact that the United States has to deal with a highly imperfect, multicultural international community but currently does not want to do so by dynamically projecting its power abroad. Hence the need for Americans to try to deal with a multipolar in-ternational environment that, admittedly, is unnervingly unpredictable.

Often overlooked, especially in the U.S. Congress, the key point is that the extent to which the United States should treat the PRC with the respect owed to a major world power depends not only on the extent to which the PRC modernizes and is willing to abide by the rules of the world system but also on the extent to which the United States is will-ing to project its military-diplomatic power abroad. The United States cannot both drastically shrink down its military capabilities and impose its rules of domestic and international behavior on the PRC. It cannot both act as though history has come to an end and expect to shape the course of history in east Asia.

Yet our recommendation to nurture a relation of mutual respect with the PRC also reflects a certain optimism which is rather widely shared around the globe, and which is only connoted by most current writing. The very concept of "Chinese culture" is rejected by many scholars as too broad and vague, but, in fact, centuries of interaction between the Chinese and other people have generated a widespread faith that there is a certain Chinese cultural mainstream, that it is basically pacific, that the Chinese people will respond constructively to a friendly international environment, and that they indeed will join "the world system." Such a constructive Chinese cultural tendency seems to underlie three of the new realities we have adduced—the recent transformation of the PRC, that of the ROC, and that of the relation between them. As Huntington has recently noted, the world's disparate cultural patterns will long persist. Yet these patterns do not all incline toward aggressive political behavior. At the very least, their international reputations in this regard differ considerably.

To be sure, because great uncertainties are associated with any cultural pattern, any dependence on some posited cultural tendency precludes an international order with guaranteed stability. It is reassuring to know, however, that, along with the dangerous uncertainties of life in a multicultural, multipolar world, at least some cultural tendencies offer some grounds for hope.

True enough, not a few Americans realistically fear that, if the PRC becomes a modern, militarily powerful nation, its policies might threaten vital U.S. interests. But what can be done today about this danger? Some contemplate applying to the PRC the policy George F. Kennan called "containment." Yet this would not be prudent until it became clear that the PRC was unwilling to join the world system and indeed was determined to threaten vital U.S. interests. That is not the situation today, when PRC foreign policy at worst is ambiguous, at best, inclined toward participation in the world system. Moreover, even a policy of partial containment would require a more forceful projection of U.S. power abroad than the American public today would accept.

If, however, a punitive policy of containment is not advisable today, how should Americans plan for the probability that China, by the middle of the twenty-first century, shall have become a modern, militarily powerful nation gifted with a talented population four times as big as the United States and animated by the belief in China's global centrality, the determination, as Sun Yat-sen put it, to "surpass Europe and America"?

Surely one pillar of our policy will have to be a continuing effort to integrate China into the world system along the lines indicated above. It is also clear that this effort must entail a great expansion of the Chinese diaspora, the many Chinese communities and networks outside China that serve as a bridge between Chinese society and the rest of the international community. China's leadership will become increasingly parochial, nationalistic, and hostile to the United States unless a large portion of its elite starts resembling Taiwan's today, a cosmopolitan group enriched by the experience of living and learning abroad. To cite the imagery in the famous Chinese television series "River Elegy," China must become less landlocked, more part of the intercourse of the maritime world. The United States, therefore, has a vital interest in seeing to it that the already large number of Chinese students in U.S. universities today become part of a ever-increasing trend. At the same time, however, the American public must become gradually educated to understand the need for a strong U.S. presence in the Pacific. It would be utopianism of the silliest kind to imagine that a world system peacefully incorporating China can flourish just on the basis of goodwill and mutual respect between nations. The relation between the West and Eurasia has long been stormy and has not yet been stabilized. What Hans J. Morgenthau called "realism" will be as needed in the future as it is today.[17]

As already indicated, the two authors of this introduction have presented this argument as a way of weaving together the variety of points made by all the conference participants, and, indeed, much in the following chapters overlaps our thesis. We cannot, however, claim that our argument directly reflects an outlook shared by all the participants. Each of their chapters probes further into the issues we have just discussed and stands on its own. (With regard to the romanization of Chinese words, each chapter uses the system favored by its author.)

Notes

1. The writers of this introduction are indebted to Michael S. Bernstam, Charles Hill, Alex Inkeles, and Abraham Sofaer for illuminating comments on various aspects of it, but none of latter is responsible for its content.

2. Record of remarks made orally at the conference by Ambassador Richard H. Solomon. All statements in the Introduction ascribed to him are taken from this record.

3. In this volume, the government ruling Taiwan is variously referred to as "Taiwan," "Republic of China," "ROC," or "The Republic of China on Taiwan." Some scholars object to the use of "Republic of China" on the grounds that official U.S. communications avoid this term, but the principles of scholarship need not coincide with those of U.S. foreign policy. The U.S. decision not to treat the ROC as a sovereign government is not necessarily a diplomatic mistake, but it should not be confused with an objective, scholarly judgment that the government in Taiwan is not a sovereign power with the right to name itself.

4. On the "inhibited center," see Introduction, by Thomas A. Metzger and Ramon H. Myers to Ramon H. Myers, ed., *Two Societies in Opposition: The Republic of China and the People's Republic of China after Forty Years* (Stanford: Hoover Institution Press, 1991), pp.xvi–xx.

5. On fiscal decentralization in the PRC today, see Yingyi Qian and Barry R. Weingast, *China's Transition to Markets: Market-Preserving Federalism, Chinese Style*, published by Hoover Institution Press as part of its Essays in Public Policy series (1995), and Albert Park, Scott Rozelle, and Changqing Ren, "Distributional Consequences of Reforming Local Public Finance in China: Fiscal Crisis in Shaanxi Province's Poor Countries" (unpublished).

6. Merle Goldman, *Sowing the Seeds of Democracy* (Cambridge, Mass.: Harvard University Press, 1994).

7. Pei Minxin, *From Reform to Revolution* (Cambridge, Mass.: Harvard University Press, 1994).

8. Ramon H. Myers, "The Socialist Market Economy in the People's Republic of China: Fact or Fiction?" The Fifty-fifth Morrison Lecture, Australian National University (November 8, 1994)(in press).

9. Samuel P. Huntington, *The Third Wave: Democratization in the Late Twentieth Century* (Norman and London: University of Oklahoma Press, 1991), pp.174–81.

10. Update of December 21, 1994, from the East-West Center: Mark J.

Valencia, "South China Sea Talks Test Asia's New Order."

11. Brett C. Lippencott, *Backgrounder,* no. 243 (March 29, 1995) (Heritage Foundation).

12. Ibid.

13. Sarah C. M. Paine, "Conflicting Empires: The Myths of Russo-Chinese Border Reflections," in Working Paper series in International Studies, Hoover Institution, Stanford University, I-94-11.

14. Conversation in May 1995 with Michael S. Bernstam.

15. See, for example, Thomas A. Metzger, "The Chinese Reconciliation of Moral-Sacred Values with Modern Pluralism," in Myers, ed., *Two Societies in Opposition*, p. 27.

16. John Dunn, *Western Political Theory in the Face of the Future* (Cambridge, Eng.: Cambridge University Press, 1993), p. 57.

17. On the thought of Morgenthau, see Robert J. Myers, "Speaking Truth to Power: The Quest for Equality in Freedom," *Society* 29, no. 2 (January–February 1992): 65–71.

CHAPTER 1

"Crossing the River by Feeling One's Way along the Bottom Stone by Stone": China's Greater China Strategy

JAMES R. LILLEY

I n dealing with China, as with everything else, most generalizations are false. The Western saying that "empires wax and wane" echoes the Chinese *fen jiu bi he, he jiu bi fen* (the disunity of the empire must be followed by unification, and vice versa), found in *The Romance of the Three Kingdoms*, a traditional Chinese literary masterpiece. Although it could just be another frequently used but false generalization, empires do in fact grow and collapse. But I for one am not presumptuous enough to say what is going to happen in China. I am going to tell you what I think has happened and perhaps why, and this is only one man's interpretation.

Going back to the late 1970s in China, Guangdong moved one step ahead (*Guangdong xian zou yi bu*) in a process of economic cooperation between southern China and Hong Kong. There was increasing interdependence between these two entities, especially in the economic field, and some China specialists began to conceptualize the huge economic potential of the links between China's southern coast and the Chinese diaspora. The economic systems were complementary, with Hong Kong moving inevitably toward economic integration with China. Later, in 1987, there was the opening up between Taiwan and China, again driven by the dynamism of economic interdependence, which came to dominate the relationship between Taiwan and China. Indicative of this economic cooperation, China had agreed earlier (1986) to Taiwan's remaining in the Asian Development Bank (albeit under considerable international pressure and insisting that this agreement would not be a precedent). Yet for the first time in a significant international governmental organization, China accepted that Taiwan could represent itself under the right nomenclature as an official organization. This was the "Chinese Taipei" formula. Seeking to bring about a "greater China," China was moving ahead with the economic integration of the mainland with both Hong Kong and Taiwan. In China's view this would lead to the political integration of Hong Kong as stated by the 1984 joint agreement between the British and the Chinese on the restoration of Chinese sovereignty over Hong Kong. China hoped for some kind of a similar movement in the political process between Taiwan and China. Things were looking good for China.

In 1989 three developments took place that changed this picture. First, China became isolated and defensive after the massacre at Tiananmen Square. Foreign tourism dropped to an all-time low. International financial institution loans stopped, and investment dropped. The Japanese third yen loan package was delayed, and Chinese economic conditions deteriorated as Premier Li Peng's economic retrenchment program took effect. Second, after Tiananmen, while foreigners held back, Taiwan and Hong Kong moved economically into China. This was a great boon to the weakened Chinese economy. Its two Chinese partners—Taiwan and Hong Kong—had rescued China in its hour of need, pouring in investment, tourism, and trade. Third, and contrary to China's desires, Taiwan and Hong Kong moved politically away from China. The arrival of Governor Chris Patten in Hong Kong stirred up a nascent Hong Kong democratic movement. A leading democratic force, Martin Lee's political organization, won a significant victory in the 1991 legislative council elections in Hong Kong. China apparently had not anticipated these disturbing factors. A politically rocky road replaced the prospect of a smooth economic integration with Hong Kong. In Taiwan, there was the rise of the Democratic Progressive Party (DPP) with an independence theme, largely driven by domestic forces but nevertheless expressing the deep convictions of the leaders of the DPP. Their commitment to a Taiwan independent of China had been punished by the Taiwan authorities with years of isolation in jails and exile. Hardened and embittered, they had come back and formed a legitimate political party in Taiwan. In their outspoken struggle to press ahead with Taiwan's democratization, they were getting an increasing slice of the electorate.

Meanwhile, in the United States and elsewhere outside China, the rise of the greater China economic concept seized the imagination of the academics and merchants. There was an illusion of economic integration leading to eventual political absorption. Leading U.S. businesspeople with Chinese backgrounds confidently pushed this theme. A rash of articles, books, and conferences in the United States dealt with the concept of a greater China.

In April 1992 the (ROC) Foundation for Exchange across the Taiwan Strait and the (PRC) Association for the Relations across the Taiwan Strait held highly symbolic talks in Singapore. Although there was some concrete progress, there were also clear limitations. But for China it was still economics in command, and a game plan was emerging. The Chinese believed that they could deal with the pro-China billionaires of Hong Kong and render these people more dependent on China. Hong Kong elite like Robert Kwok, Li Ka-hsing, Henry Fok, and Stanley Ho all had strong economic links with China and could handle Martin Lee, Christine Lo, Emily Lau, and Szetu Wah. China's strategy was to use economic leverage to put down the opposition politicians. In the case of Taiwan, China tried to induce people like the executives of Formosa Plastics, Evergreen, and President Enterprises to make major investments into China. Thus Taiwanese capitalists were being lured into China, while China was trying to give them the message that China and Taiwan could move forward with the *san tong*—the three direct links—to Taiwan's economic benefit. China's leaders were hoping that these influential Taiwanese would check the influence of the extremist political views in the opposition party.

China felt comfortable enough with this strategy in 1992 to begin focusing its growing military power on the South China Sea rather than against Taiwan. China sensed a certain vulnerability in the South China Sea, given the numerous conflicting claims and diverse national interests in that area. Also the United States was clearly going to pull out of its Subic Bay base in the Philippines. In February 1992, the National People's Congress passed a law on China's territorial waters and islands in the South China Sea and elsewhere reiterating China's right to use force in these areas. This law took in not only the Spratly and Paracel Islands but all the water around them and between them. It also involved the Senkaku Islands claimed by Japan and Taiwan.

The Chinese backed this law up with a growing and modernizing military. They put priority on naval and air power with an emphasis on power projection. They were developing a rapid deployment force of roughly one hundred thousand troops ("fist troops," as the Chinese call them). They purchased the advanced fighter bomber, the SU-27, from Russia; began building more major surface combatant and replenishment ships; and obtained Kilo-class submarines from Russia. (The acquisitions from Russia were a bonanza that was both cheap and modern.) There were also reports that China was recruiting Russian engineers, technicians, and scientists involved in guidance systems for intermediate range ballistic missiles and propulsions for nuclear submarines. China during this period also demonstrated a willingness to use force against Vietnam. In 1988 China won a shootout in which it gave Vietnam a lesson on the seas. There were other incidents in 1992 and 1994.

China, however, was beginning to run into problems with the Association of Southeast Asian Nations (ASEAN) on its territorial claims and on its power projection. ASEAN members, including Singapore, Malaysia, Indonesia, Brunei, Thailand, and to a lesser degree the Philippines were beginning to offer the United States facilities to support a continued U.S. presence. No bases were involved, but there were shipyards in Indonesia and Malaysia—Malaysia was repairing C-130s, Singapore was offering facilities for Westpaclog, a U.S. naval logistics support unit. There were continuing joint exercises including Singapore, Indonesia, and Thailand. Many of these countries were buying U.S.-made F-16 aircraft; Malaysia was buying F-18s. In addition to joint maneuvering, personnel exchanges, planning and command conferences, there was a movement toward interoperability of conventional forces. The Filipinos, out of sync with the rest of ASEAN, were forcing the United States to give up bases in Subic Bay and Clark Field. But even this is changing. The Filipinos are now welcoming U.S. ship visits and talking seriously about renewing joint exercises. Although the United States jumped the gun by seeking to preposition war matériel both in the Philippines and in Thailand (they both rejected it), the overall trend was to welcome the U.S. military to the area.

In the case of Taiwan, economic integration did not lead to closer political integration. The growing power of the opposition DPP reached 41 percent in the elections of 1993. There were also Chinese suspicions about the real intentions of Taiwan's president, Lee Teng-hui. Although he ostensibly supported a one-China policy, China believed, on the basis of statements Lee made in the Japanese media and elsewhere, that he was really interested in carving out greater autonomy for Taiwan.

Leading Chinese economists met in Beijing in April 1993 and agreed that, although there was increasing economic integration, it would end up with Taiwan's being treated as an equal. This was not healthy politically. Deng's concept of one country, two systems, was not working well in the case of Taiwan. As a result China backed away from any arrangement that would treat Taiwan as an equal. As this was happening, Taiwan was sending Beijing some key economic advisers, such as K. T. Lee, to provide China with macroeconomic advice on such issues as an autonomous central bank, a reliable monetary system, and credit manipulation based on economic, not political, grounds. Taiwan was also giving advice on how to build efficient container ports and set up infrastructure projects, as well as on macroeconomic policy. Discussions were going on between the top Chinese political leadership and key Taiwan businessmen closely linked to President Lee Teng-hui. The situation between China and Taiwan was becoming increasingly complex, with contradictory currents.

Taiwan was developing its own southern strategy, diversifying its investment to avoid economic dependence on China. Taiwan became the third-largest investor in Indonesia and the largest in Vietnam. This strategy, financially supported by the Taiwan government, was designed to pull investment away from China and turn it toward Southeast Asia, thereby balancing Taiwan's investment portfolio. At the same time, Taiwan was building its military strength and becoming a more formidable defensive military power, with new Frigates, French Mirages, F-16s, and antisubmarine warfare helicopters. This, Taiwan leaders believed, would reduce the Chinese military option.

China for its part turned increasingly to Europe, the United States, and Japan for investments in the modernization of its economy, for there were limits on what overseas Chinese, Hong Kong, and Taiwan money could do. Major projects like the Three Gorges, power generation, and major infrastructure needed large Western and Japanese financial, management, and technological inputs. The United States became China's largest investor, with a 50 percent increase in 1994. The fourth Japanese yen loan package came in at $7 billion, considerably more than the third yen loan package of 1989–90, which was $5.6 billion. Both Japanese packages contained generous terms for China's major projects in terms of grace periods, grants, and low-interest loans.

The visits of Helmut Kohl of Germany, Prime Minister Chrétian of Canada, and U.S. commerce secretary Ron Brown, each one with multibillion-dollar deals with China, stressed the importance of these Western inputs. The Chinese seem to be encouraging the United States, Japan, and Europe to participate in the economic boom and playing them off against one another. China also appears interested in building a strong, modern economic base, accompanied by a selective military buildup. As Deng Xiaoping put it, "quadrupling China's gross industrial and agricultural product means that by the end of the century improving military equipment would be an easy job." Deng Xiaoping and Chen Yun allegedly watched the entire gulf war in early 1991 on CNN in Shanghai. On the basis of this exposure to the complexities of modern warfare, they decided that their strong economic base could be better accomplished with the support of Western countries. They also decided that they would have to accumulate some military expertise by renewing their military and strategic relationship with the remaining superpower, the United States.

Thus, in the view of the Chinese leadership, over the next ten to twenty years, China would become economically powerful but maintain close ties to Taiwan, Hong Kong, and Southeast Asia. Over time China's military buildup would reach a point where it could intimidate Taiwan in a credible way. To forestall any precipitous move toward independence in Taiwan, however, China conducted joint military exercises in the Taiwan Strait. Much of this was probably gong banging, but no one could afford to ignore it. In reality, China was looking at a long-term strategy (ten to twenty years) to build up its economic power and its military power projection capability so that it would become the premier military power in Asia, thus enabling it to deal more effectively with its recalcitrant Chinese *tong bao* (brothers).

In 1994 China began downplaying its military intentions in the South China Sea and making efforts to ameliorate its relations with the members of ASEAN. Jiang Zemin, during the Asian-Pacific Economic Cooperation conference in Djakarta in 1994, visited Southeast Asian nations to reassure them that Chinese intentions were peaceful and that China looked for joint exploitation of economic resources, not military confrontation. In contrast to earlier protests about other nations' drilling in its territorial seas, China has said little or nothing about the $30-billion gas deal between Indonesia and Exxon, which is off Natuna Island in the middle of territorial waters claimed by China. China also reached an agreement with Vietnam on general territorial questions including the South China Sea. Using consultation, not confrontation, as the means to work out disputes, the Chinese began to seek international, including U.S., legal help for their claims in the South China Sea. Earlier, the Vietnamese had hired Covington and Burling to support their claims, so the Chinese looked for a prestigious U.S. law firm and began to talk seriously about the problems in the South China Sea within a legal context rather than a military one. Finally, in the ASEAN Regional Forum, the Chinese participated on sovereignty and security issues, stressing that the National People's Congress law was just that—law, not policy. The Chinese began to talk frequently and seriously with Taiwan representatives in international nongovernmental organizations involving security and sovereignty in the South China Sea.

Previously, they had often refused to attend such meetings when Taiwan was present or had attended with a second-rate team.

This shift in the Chinese position is consistent with a rational Chinese foreign policy. In Chinese foreign policy, there has often been a struggle between the so-called nationalistic, anti-imperialistic, anticolonial line and the pragmatic international line. This confrontation came to a head when China had to choose between supporting the Khmer Rouge in Cambodia and going along with the solution proposed by the five permanent members of the U.N. Security Council. China chose to go along with the Security Council's solution in Cambodia, thus siding against their so-called socialist ally, the pariah Pol Pot. Similarly, in Desert Storm, China's old Third World partner and collaborator Saddam Hussein, to whom China sold billions of dollars of weapons during the Iran-Iraq war (China also sold weapons to Iran), presented China with a dilemma. China could have stood by Saddam in his struggle against "Western imperialist encroachment," for he was a Third World leader who had taken on the United States in Saudi Arabia. But China opted to go against Saddam, following the U.N. consortium led by the United States. This was not only a significant but a quick decision: starting in August 1990, China voted for eleven resolutions in the U.N. Security Council to punish Saddam with sanctions—this at the same time that the United States was still sanctioning China for Tiananmen—another victory for the internationalists.

China now faces a major foreign policy dilemma closer to home. Although still offering verbal support to North Korea, China is beginning to use its influence and leverage to seek a denuclearization of the peninsula as well as economic reform of North Korea. At the same time, China is moving toward a closer collaboration with South Korea and away from its old Korean socialist comrade-in-arms. China, aware that its interests lie with the winner, South Korea, is playing an increasingly constructive role consistent with what the United States and its allies are trying to accomplish—namely, peace, stability, prosperity, and no weapons of mass destruction in North Korea. This is a profound change from China's policy of total support for North Korea in the 1950s, 1960s, and 1970s. China again is siding with the international consortium, not its Third World ally. This could also be true in the

South China Sea and in Taiwan if the United States plays its cards right. China obviously acts in its own interests, but in case after case its interests are becoming closer to prevailing international views.

All this is happening at a time of leadership transition and succession in China, which makes decisions even more complex and difficult for the Chinese. The tectonic plates have been shifting in China. The movement from autarky to interdependence has taken place in twenty short years between 1973 and 1993. This has been accompanied by huge shifts in population toward the coast, with increasing disparities in income that have caused major social problems for the regime in its rapid economic modernization. To complicate things further, there are large statistical distortions. In the Chinese system no one is sure how fast the floating population is growing or how big the problems caused by this are because Chinese statistics often are false. Thus problems can be hard to pin down. Overseas Chinese business leaders are becoming more outspoken about the problems of doing business in China, mainly because of the lack of predictability in the systems. Foreign participants in joint ventures complain about cooked books, a lack of reliability, and a failure of confidence.

China has also had to deal with the results of the Taiwan elections of December 3, 1994. A basically responsible democratic vote in Taiwan did not support an independence policy. The opposition candidate, Chen Shui-pien, was elected by a minority in Taipei City, and issues such as KMT corruption and nepotism played a more important role in Chen's victory than did independence. The pro-one-China New Party also split the vote, hurting the KMT. Taiwan understandably wants international legitimacy but so far has been responsible in seeking it. It is important that the Chinese not only understand but also encourage this.

The Chinese are showing some creative signs of change. Judging from a recent *Wall Street Journal* article, Zhou Nan, the head of China News Agency in Hong Kong, sounds somewhat like Newt Gingrich in his call for reductions in government spending, reductions of pensions, and welfare reform in Hong Kong. Zhou is still for tight political control but with reduced government spending. In contrast, the opposition democratic elements in Hong Kong have come out for increased government spending and broadening the democratic base. Zhou's comments were more in line with the billionaire fat cats of Hong Kong than with the toiling masses.

As for China itself, mixed signals from the internal scene are emerging. There seem to be differences in the Chinese leadership on such issues as economic flexibility and domestic change. A leadership group at the center appears to emphasize the separation of the party and the government, the enlarging of the socialist "bird cage," more rapid cuts in subsidies to state-owned enterprises, and expansion of the rule of law. At the Fourteenth National Party Congress (NPC) in October 1993, the party solidified its hold on the core of high government positions but did not succeed in expanding its grassroots support. Later, the party tried to remedy this but still seemed to concentrate its influence in government at the highest levels.

Qiao Shi, the chairman of the NPC, has repeatedly stressed strengthening the legal system, stating that the next five years of the Eighth NPC were crucial for this. The highest priority is economic legislation. Enforcing the constitution became the responsibility of the National People's Congress, in Qiao Shi's view.

During increased contacts between the NPC and the U.S. Congress, key members of the NPC told members of Congress that they had discarded many of President Clinton's earlier harsh statements against China as just so much campaign rhetoric. These people said repeatedly that their laws within China should converge with international laws and that they should draw on other countries' legal systems. China has joined the Missile Technology Control Regime, the Nuclear Nonproliferation Treaty, and the Berne Convention on intellectual property rights and has participated actively in international antidrug campaigns. Although dominating the Asian Games in Hiroshima, China dealt responsibly with the drug problem among its athletes. In other words, the Chinese are integrating their system with the world system.

But these more flexible Chinese leaders have to be careful not to make Zhao Ziyang's mistake of trying hurriedly to reform the political system. Rather, they support Deng's theory of building socialism with Chinese characteristics. These Chinese leaders talk repeatedly about the rule of law, mainly because it helps prevent chaos and can institutionalize the reform process. They support a rule of law backed up by strong security forces, but they want a constitution that is a legal instrument, not a bludgeon to punish dissidents without due process.

Leftists on the attack are evident in China. Deng himself cites leftist interference as one of the three major problems—the others being localism and corruption. Yang Shangkun has joined Deng in attacking the leftists, who, Yang says, are for slower growth.

While PRC leaders are moving ahead on linking China to the international system, they are also taking care of the People's Liberation Army by passing laws that support military service of officers on active duty and regulations governing officers of rank. They have considerably increased the military budget and approved extensive purchases of modern foreign equipment and technology. NPC staffers regularly comment that the State Council should draft less legislation and the NPC more. (The mix is about 70 percent to 30 percent in favor of the State Council now.) NPC staffers complain about this, insisting that the drafting procedures should move over to the NPC. The NPC, reportedly, is starting its own newspaper, the *Renmin zhishang bao*. NPC members and staffers are also trying to depoliticize the central bank. They are passing a labor law, which might be just waste paper, but they are also trying to pass a "sunshine law" to deal with corruption among party cadres.

In a characteristic Chinese balancing act, Ye Xuan Ping, a noted reformer in Guangdong, has been promoted along with Qin Jiwei, a military law and order man—both can now attend the Politburo meetings. Another reformer, Hu Qili, has been elevated along with Zhang Wannian, a leading military man who is highly regarded by U.S. Defense Department officials. So Hu Qili and Ye Xuan Ping are moving up in parallel with the two military men, Qin Jiwei and Zhang Wannian.

Recently Peng Zhen, Chen Yun, and Song Ping have been more active. Two of these are known hard-liners. Peng is a rule-of-law man and a strong backer of Qiao Shi's efforts to create a legal structure for China. On TV Peng reminded people that he ranks Deng in the party.

There may, therefore, be a more flexible faction emerging within the Chinese communist leadership. Characteristics of this faction could be rule of law under the auspices of the NPC, led by Qiao Shi, with a focus on economic issues.

It is important for the United States to recognize this trend early. Some U.S. leaders recognized Deng Xiaoping as a potential leader of economic reform when he came back into the system in the 1972–73 period, although, at that time, he was only a vice premier. By 1974 George Bush, then head of United States Liaison Organisation in Beijing, had spotted Deng as a man who would become an economic reformer and probably the eventual ruler in China. Even when Deng fell in 1976, the United States had faith in him. By 1978, Deng had returned and initiated his major economic reforms at the Eleventh Party Plenum in November 1978, which led to the major economic developments in China today. Deng was a political dogmatist but an economic pragmatist. It was important that the United States bet on him early because he led the normalization of relations with the United States.

Today some influential people in China are moving in directions that are compatible with U.S. interests. Although the outlines of what China might become remain murky, out of the mist and the shadows certain forms are emerging. It is important that we recognize these forms now, as the process of change is likely to be turbulent and protracted. A consistent and coherent U.S. position could be one important factor in influencing a favorable outcome.

CHAPTER 2

The Republic of China and People's Republic of China Relationship: The Unification Issue

RAMON H. MYERS

Since 1978 the United States has formally recognized the People's Republic of China (PRC) as China and maintained informal relations with the Republic of China (ROC) on Taiwan, referring to that entity merely as Taiwan. While adhering to the principle of one China, according to which Taiwan is a part of China, the United States also has emphasized that any unification should be peaceful. This standpoint, however, leaves many questions unanswered. How, for instance, should the United States respond when the ROC, contradicting the PRC, seeks to join the international community and participate in organizations like the General Agreement on Tariffs and Trade (GATT), Asia-Pacific Economic Cooperation (APEC), and the United Nations? How should the United States deal with the recent revival of tensions between the two Chinese states? After long advocating the democratization of the ROC, can the United States watch the twenty-one million people of Taiwan carry out democratization and then ignore their aspirations? To complicate matters more, what should the United States do if a majority of the Taiwan people reject the principle of one China? This possibility hinges not only on PRC-ROC relations but also on the feelings and hopes of Taiwan's people who have links with other countries and want them improved.

In an effort to better understand these issues, I first review the history of U.S. policy with regard to the issue of Chinese unification and then reflect on the origins of the new tensions between the PRC and the ROC. I then discuss how these tensions endanger U.S. interests in greater China and how the United States should deal with this danger.

The Evolution of U.S. Policy regarding Unification

Between 1950 and 1978, the United States recognized the Republic of China as the sovereign government of China, provided it with military and economic assistance, and treated the China problem as a confrontation between freedom and totalitarianism. Yet, seeking to keep that confrontation peaceful, the United States used its power and influence to persuade the ROC not to initiate any conflict with the PRC. Conversely, it intervened to prevent the PRC from attacking the ROC.

After 1972, however, U.S. relations with the PRC improved, leading to détente and the normalization of diplomatic relations between the two countries. The United States agreed with the ROC and the PRC that Taiwan was part of China and that China's unification was a problem to be resolved by the Chinese people. The United States expressed the hope that unification would be peaceful but indicated no intention to intervene should the PRC use force to achieve it. The United States continued to be interested in keeping the confrontation between the ROC and the PRC peaceful, not only using its PRC connection in its own confrontation with the USSR but also continuing to offer the ROC some measure of support.

This was a difficult balancing act. The U.S. Congress passed the Taiwan Relations Act on January 1, 1979, to strengthen U.S.-ROC ties, thus angering the Beijing regime. In 1982 the PRC and U.S. governments agreed to a communiqué that would phase out weapons sales to the ROC, disappointing the Taiwan regime. In 1992 the Bush administration supplied advanced weapons to the ROC to balance military power across the Taiwan Strait, angering the PRC. In October 1994 the

U.S. government passed a law allowing high ROC and U.S. officials to interact more closely, again infuriating Beijing's leaders.

However difficult this balancing act may have been, it was facilitated by the agreement among all three parties that Taiwan, in one sense or another, was part of China. This agreement has its roots in the complex history of ROC-PRC relations.

PRC-ROC Relations

From 1927 until 1949 the China mainland was engulfed in a conflict between two political parties who disagreed about how China should be modernized. These were the Chinese Communist Party (CCP) and the Kuomintang (KMT). After the CCP defeated the KMT in 1949, the KMT retreated to Taiwan. From then on, the two Chinese states, ruled by these single parties, competed for the right to represent China in the world order. Both parties insisted on the principle of one China and held that Taiwan was a part of China. Until 1972 most nations recognized the ROC on Taiwan as China. After 1972 the pendulum swung the other way, and a majority of nations recognized the PRC as China. While competing for the international legitimacy to be recognized as China, the two Chinese states governed their territories very differently but still pursued their goal of unifying China.

The CCP rejected modernizing China's traditional economic marketplace and instead established a centrally planned economy based on collective organizations and state-managed enterprises. The KMT's preference for modernizing Taiwan's economic marketplace to include extensive private property rights, freedom to produce and buy, and markets for production and exchange, helped by generous U.S. economic and military aid in the 1950s, soon produced prosperity and a vibrant civil society. The PRC's centrally planned socialism, however, produced an unproductive economy in which living standards stagnated after the early 1950s.

Two further developments made the two Chinese societies very different. The CCP insisted on regulating an ideological marketplace to prevent other ideas from challenging Marxism, Leninism, and Mao Tse-tung's thought. It also monopolized political power and ruled through enormous state power, in effect behaving as a totalitarian regime.

The KMT allowed an ideological marketplace in which Western liberal democratic principles competed with Sun Yat-sen's Three Principles of the People and Confucianism but did not tolerate Marxism and socialist thought. It also promoted a limited democracy; in the spring of 1986 Chiang Ching-kuo, the KMT's leader, initiated political reform and on July 15, 1987, lifted martial law. These actions signaled Taiwan's democratization, which has been smooth and peaceful until the present.

After 1980 the CCP began liberalizing China's economic marketplace; by the mid-1990s the government's totalitarian grip on ideas and political power had begun to relax. The PRC's leaders wanted to preserve CCP political dominance but develop a socialist type of market economy. The CCP, unable to regulate ideas as before, has even begun to allow village leaders and councils to be elected.

Although experiencing very different modernization paths, the PRC and the ROC competed for international legitimacy. Both Chinese states adhered to the one-China principle and refused other states the right of dual recognition of both China states. Each claimed sovereignty over the other. Therefore, the foreign policies of the two Chinese states differed from those of the divided Korean and German states. Most countries maintained dual diplomatic relations with both Korean and both German states, and none of those divided states claimed sovereignty over its rival.

After 1980, however, the ROC-PRC military rivalry diminished, and Beijing's leaders repeatedly made conciliatory proposals to the ROC government, urging direct negotiations between the CCP and KMT and adopting a formula for unifying the two territories and their peoples. The PRC proposed formula, based on the framework used to integrate Hong Kong and the mainland after British rule terminated on July 1, 1997, called for a "one-country, two-system" formula that would grant Taiwan's people their system of governance and military force in exchange for acknowledging PRC sovereignty over Taiwan and representing Taiwan in the international order. In other words, Taiwan was to become a province of the PRC with special status.

Although Taiwan's leaders rejected Beijing's overtures, military tensions across the Taiwan Strait continued to diminish. In 1987 a breakthrough occurred when both states agreed to allow travel, followed by trade and investment, between the two territories. By September 1993 Taiwan's investment in mainland China had risen to US$16.8 billion compared with US$3.5 billion in 1991.[1] By October 1994, Taiwan's exports to mainland China were roughly 10.8 percent of its exports to the world market, indicating the island's growing dependency on that huge market.[2]

To facilitate this expanding relationship, in late 1990 both states agreed to establish nonofficial organizations to discuss illegal immigration and postal exchange as well as other issues related to trade and investment. So far, both Chinese states have held three nonofficial meetings. At the same time, the harshness exemplified in the ROC approach to the PRC dramatically softened.

For example, in April 1991 the ROC renounced its state of war with the communist regime, initiated in 1947, and declared that it would never use force to unify China. Similarly, the ROC published a blueprint for achieving China's peaceful unification: the first stage would create trust and mutual respect, paving the way for the second stage, in which postal, air, and sea communications between the two territories would be established; in the final stage, long- term negotiations would eventually agree on a framework for unification. This blueprint was predicated on both sides renouncing the use of force, treating each other as equal partners, achieving a high level of economic prosperity and relative equal distribution of wealth, and relying on democratic procedures for the Chinese people to express their preference about unification.

In 1993, the ROC government modified its foreign policy further to accommodate Taiwan's democratic transitions. Sensitive to Taiwan's international isolation, ROC leaders began visiting countries in Southeast Asia and Latin America to build support for upgrading diplomatic relations with the ROC and supporting its demands to enter international organizations of which it formerly was a member like the United Nations.

In July 1994 the ROC issued a White Paper acknowledging that the PRC possessed sovereign authority over the Chinese mainland, including

Tibet, something it had never before conceded. At the same time, it insisted that the ROC possessed sovereignty over Taiwan and its offshore islands. Although the ROC still adhered to the principle of one China, this new interpretation denoted two political entities. The ROC informed other nations that it welcomed their dual recognition of both Chinese states, a position it had rejected in the past. The ROC thus tried to turn its confrontation with the PRC into a peacefully competitive relationship between two states, each of which respected the other's sovereignty.

The PRC rejected the ROC's new formulation of the one-China principle and has blocked its efforts to join the international community. In August 1993, the PRC published a White Paper claiming that Taiwan had always been part of China; that Taiwan, with the assistance of the United States, had been occupied by an illegal regime in 1949; and that the people of China wanted Taiwan united with the PRC. The PRC again proposed the formula first offered in 1980, the "one country with two different systems." Finally, the PRC insisted on the right to use military force if the people and government on Taiwan rejected the principle of one China and established a Republic of Taiwan.

Thus, the one-China position, long agreed on by both, was now interpreted differently by the ROC. Whereas both sides had always rejected dual recognition by other nations, the ROC now welcomed it. Whereas the ROC had once accepted its international isolation, it now vigorously strived to acquire some "international space."

The ROC changed its policy toward unification in part because Taiwan's democratization had provoked heated debates about China's unification and how to reverse the ROC's isolation in the international community. Democracy also gave impetus to Taiwanese nationalism. Taiwan's democratization had also reformed the 1947 constitution, removed mainlanders from controlling political power, expanded national elections for Taiwan's leaders and representatives, established a free public media, and guaranteed personal liberties, making it possible for a native-born Taiwanese generation of leaders to acquire political power. The KMT's first Taiwanese chairman, Lee Teng-hui, realized that the KMT could only win voter support if it charted a new foreign policy calling for China's unification and legitimating the status of the ROC in the international community.

The old KMT leadership, made up of mainlanders, shared a dream of unifying Taiwan and mainland China under the 1947 constitution and Sun Yat-sen's Three Principles of the People, but the CCP's dictatorial control over the mainland made that impossible. To realize the dream of unifying China, Chiang Ching-kuo and the KMT had promoted democracy in Taiwan. But as democracy developed, it encouraged great debate about the future governance of Taiwan. Taiwanese nationalism soon became a potent force.

Before 1945 Taiwan had undergone fifty years of Japanese rule during which many elite had been Japanized and a large number of people had come to respect Japanese organizational efficiency and industrial-urban development. Thus, when the Nationalist government took over Taiwan from imperial Japan on October 25, 1945, its officials were ill prepared to administer a Chinese society long accustomed to Japanese ways. Poorly prepared and few in number, Nationalist troops and officials had only partly rebuilt the economy before grievances between mainlanders and Taiwanese snowballed, culminating in the February 28, 1947, uprising that lasted two weeks before Nationalist troops from the mainland arrived to brutally suppress it.[3] This event left a legacy of hatred toward the new regime and spawned an overseas movement of Taiwanese nationalism whose leaders were dedicated to destroying the Nationalist government on Taiwan and replacing it by a Taiwanese administration.

Thereafter, the Nationalist government, using a mix of repression and reform, allowed local elections but suppressed any attempt to establish political parties. In these decades the KMT nurtured a limited democracy and a small political opposition that gradually learned how to play by the rules. But among the political opposition were those who remembered the Nationalist repression of the February 28, 1947, uprising and the arrests of anyone who criticized the government in the 1950s. Many of these critics were arrested and imprisoned by the KMT regime and, on their release, joined the political opposition and later the Democratic Progressive Party (DPP) that had been allowed to form in September 1986. One critic, Shih Ming-te, who had spent several decades in prison, became the party's chairman. The DPP became split between prodemocratizers and Taiwanese nationalists who wanted a new constitution and a Republic of Taiwan. So far, the prodemocratizers have managed to impose moderation on the DPP leadership, but the Taiwanese nationalists are still a powerful force in that party.

Democratization also promoted heated discussions in society about Taiwan's identity and fostered Taiwanese nationalism, defined as a movement seeking a national identity by emphasizing the linguistic, cultural, and historical distinctiveness of Taiwanese and trying to establish Taiwan as a sovereign democratic republic without any special relation with China. A poll taken in early 1995 showed that only 10 percent of the people want an independent Taiwan.[4] But unpredictable events can change that sentiment. On March 31, 1994, twenty-four Taiwanese tourists were murdered in a strange boating incident on Chientao Lake in Chekiang Province on the mainland. Although mainland officials tried to cover up the event, eventually three young people were arrested, tried, and executed for slaying the passengers. But the incident seemed to have involved other individuals who were never apprehended. The alleged cover-up enraged officials and people in Taiwan. A Gallup poll conducted in Taiwan soon after the incident showed that popular feeling in support of an independent nation (Taiwan) had shot up to its highest level—27 percent—exceeding the 23.7 percent reached in 1991.[5]

In 1992 the lingering anger over the Nationalist government's handling of the February 28, 1947, uprising was finally addressed when the government established a commission to examine the causes of that tragedy and apportion blame. The commission found the government partly responsible for the tragedy. The Legislative Yuan then passed a law stipulating that the government build a memorial for the victims and pay compensation to their families. On February 28, 1995, President Lee Teng-hui unveiled the memorial and apologized, on behalf of the government, to the victims and their families, thus putting that issue to rest.

Although it is uncertain how many people living in Taiwan today support Taiwanese nationalism, it is a force to be reckoned with, as seen in the events of 1994 when tensions again increased between the Chinese states. In early spring the Chientao incident in Chekiang Province (mentioned above) enraged and frustrated many, increasing popular support for an independent Republic of Taiwan. In May President

Lee told Shima Ryotaro, a Japanese journalist, that "it was a tragedy to have been born a Taiwanese."[6] His remarks angered Beijing officials, who began to see him as a "closet" Taiwanese nationalist. The publication of the ROC's White Paper in early summer further angered Beijing's leaders, who vowed to impose sanctions on any nation that tried to upgrade relations with the ROC or support ROC entry into an international organization. With its great military force in reserve, PRC leaders continued to say that they would use that force if the people of Taiwan made any attempt to establish a political system independent from China. Meanwhile, the ROC has conducted a delicate balancing act—advocating the peaceful unification of China but insisting on expanding its international space.

Tensions across the Taiwan Straits slightly improved in early 1995 after the leaders of both states advanced proposals for resolving the impasse. On January 30, 1995, Jiang Zemin, general secretary of the CCP and the PRC's president, advanced a conciliatory eight-point proposal:

- Both sides should adhere to the principle of one China.

- Taiwan should have nongovernment ties with other states but not expand its international living space.

- Both sides should directly negotiate all issues.

- We support a peaceful unification of China, but we will use force "against the schemers of foreign forces interfering with China's reunification and trying to bring about the 'independence of Taiwan.'"

- To facilitate cooperation between both sides, both sides should negotiate to establish the three direct links as soon as possible.

- Both sides should uphold and perpetuate Chinese culture.

- Our side will respect the lifestyle of the Taiwan people.

- Taiwan's leaders are free to visit the mainland, and the Chinese people should arrange a meeting of the leaders from both sides.[7]

With calm rhetoric, Jiang Zemin tried to cool the tensions of 1994, urging that the leaders of both sides meet on Chinese territory and negotiate how to accelerate interactions between the two territories. But in fact, the PRC position toward the ROC was unchanged.

On April 8, 1995, roughly two months after Jiang's proposal, President Lee responded with the ROC's six-point proposal:

- China only can be unified only on the basis that "each of the two sides is ruled by a separate government."

- Bilateral exchanges concerning Chinese culture should be strengthened.

- Trade and economic ties should be developed into mutually beneficial and complementary relations.

- Both sides should be assured of the ability to join international organizations on an equal footing, and leaders of both sides should meet in a natural setting.

- Disputes should be peacefully resolved, and the Chinese Communists should renounce the use of force.

- Both sides should jointly safeguard prosperity and promote democracy in Hong Kong and Macao.[8]

The ROC also expressed a warm, friendly message, but its position was unchanged. As tensions seemed to ease, efforts continued between Taipei and Beijing to arrange another informal meeting in July 1995 in Beijing.

But in the summer of 1995, new events inflamed passions in Beijing. Angry at both the ROC and the United States for President Lee's visit to Cornell University in June, PRC leaders suddenly canceled the July meeting with the ROC. Military maneuvers then commenced in late July, with missiles being fired from Kiangsi Province into the ocean about eighty miles north of Taiwan. In August and September PRC newspapers severely criticized President Lee Teng-hui for trying to create an "independent" Taiwan.

To sum up, both Chinese states have ended their cold war and greatly improved their relations, but they still have not begun high-level, official negotiations. Moreover, regarding Chinese unification, they continue to disagree peacefully while trying to promote economic and cultural exchanges. Yet they have reached an impasse and fundamentally disagree on where to go from here. The present leaders in Beijing regard the ROC as a local government. Strong nationalist sentiments justify the PRC's belief that Taiwan belongs to China, despite the fact that the PRC has never governed Taiwan. The ROC insists on equivalence and mutual respect; its leaders and people now have a democracy and living standards that they want to preserve.

Around 60 percent of the people in Taiwan support their government's position toward the PRC and its foreign policy (in other words, they favor the status quo).[9] Taiwan's people want the ROC to be treated fairly by the international community; although frustrated with Beijing's interventionist tactics to isolate the ROC, they realize that new leaders will be taking power in Beijing in the near future and hope for greater flexibility from them on the China mainland-Taiwan problem.

But Taiwanese nationalism remains a small, potent force that could erupt if an unpredictable event, or series of events, revived tensions across the Taiwan Strait, as occurred in 1995. The radical extremists of the DPP will appeal to that force if the time comes. So far, the DPP politicians voted into office have behaved moderately, realizing that the voters can quickly replace them.

Meanwhile, the Taiwan problem will continue to haunt U.S. policy makers as it did in May 1995, when both branches of Congress voted that the United States should allow the ROC head of state, President Lee Teng-hui, to visit the United States and speak at his alma mater, Cornell University. The U.S. State Department refused to grant him a visa, fearing that Lee's visit would anger Beijing, but President Clinton finally approved the visa. Lee visited the United States, and Sino-American relations rapidly deteriorated. The Taiwan problem will thus continue to challenge U.S. China policy, particularly as it becomes politicized in Congress and coalitions form to attack the administration's China policy.

What Can the United States Do?

The Chinese scene today is very different from what it was fifteen years ago. ROC democratization, which the United States always championed, is now mixed with Taiwanese nationalism, which rejects the unification of China. The majority of people on Taiwan, perhaps seven or eight out of ten, are still willing to consider some form of unification but only on a long-term basis and only according to something like the British Commonwealth formula. Although the KMT ruling party adheres to the new one-China principle, it must work especially hard to stay in power, as seen from the December 2, 1995, parliamentary elections in which the KMT won only a slight majority of seats and less than 50 percent of the popular vote. If the PRC continues to isolate the ROC and if Taiwanese society begins to divide, the KMT will find it increasingly difficult to uphold its one-China principle.

Peaceful, stable, economically strong relations between both Chinese states are in the interest of all concerned, including the United States, but tensions across the Taiwan Strait have revived in late 1995. The majority want to cooperate with the PRC and maintain the status quo on both sides of the Taiwan Strait, but prudence is required from both states.

Meanwhile, what can the United States and Japan do to ensure the status quo?

They can encourage both Chinese parties to renounce force and gradually discuss their differences and resolve them through cooperation and compromise. The Clinton administration and the Republican-dominated Congress should discuss with Japan, the ROC, and the PRC how to achieve this goal.[10]

As in the past, the Clinton administration should continually review its China policy by

- Conducting military assessments of the balance of military power in greater China, especially across the Taiwan Strait

- Taking measures to restore that balance, should it now favor the PRC, by quickly supplying the ROC with advanced

weapons at bargain prices to deal with future PRC naval
blockage and/or military threat of attack

Finally, U.S. policy makers should try to persuade Beijing to
renounce the use of force to achieve the unification of China and agree
to discussions with Taipei on how to establish cooperation in order to
build a special relationship based on mutual trust. Even if the PRC
symbolically retained the right to use force, it could make clear its decision to avoid the use of force, agreeing, for instance, to some demilitarization of the Taiwan Strait. The demilitarization of Kinmen and
Matsu could also be considered.

A commitment to a peaceful resolution of the China unification
issue by both Chinese states could enhance mutual trust between the
two sides. Furthermore, every effort should be made to convince the
PRC to respect the ROC's democracy, so that the two Chinese states
can agree to negotiate a unification framework based on the commonwealth principle.

That new arrangement would ensure the separate governance of
each Chinese state but enable each state to cooperate as one China
without dividing China. Such a unification formula would allow both
Chinese states to participate in international organizations on terms on
which terms both sides agree. The PRC would respect Taiwan's political system. In return the ROC would work closely with the PRC to
modernize the mainland, and both would cooperate in international
affairs in the interests of preserving the integrity of one China in the
world order.

Notes

1. Ramon H. Myers and Linda Chao, "Cross-Strait Economic Relations and Their Implications for Taiwan," *Issues & Studies* 30, no. 12 (December 1994): 98.
2. Commission on Mainland Affairs, Executive Yuan, *Liang-an ching-chi t'ung-chi yüeh-pao* (Monthly economic statistics on the cross straits' relationship) 29 (January 1995): 30.
3. For an account of this uprising, see Lai Tse-han, Ramon H. Myers, and Wei Wou, *A Tragic Beginning: The Taiwan Uprising of February 28, 1947* (Stanford: Stanford University Press, 1991).
4. Li Ta-wei and Ch'iu Yuan-pin, "Min-i sui-juh liu-shui, pu-liu hsiang wai-jen-tien" (Although public opinion is not very stable, it still prefers the status quo) *Chung-kuo shih-pao chou-k'an* (China times weekly) 164 (February 19–25, 1995): 21.
5. See the results of a Gallup poll in *Chung-kuo shih-pao* (China times) (Taipei), April 18, 1994, p. 2.
6. See the Shima–President Lee interview in "Basho no kurushimi: Taiwan jin ni umareta hiai" (Taiwan's agony: The tragedy of having been born a Taiwanese) *Shukan Asahi* (The Asahi weekly) May 6–13, 1994, pp. 42–49.
7. Jiang Zemin, "Continue to Promote the Reunification of the Motherland," *Foreign Broadcast Information Service*, China-95-019, January 30, 1995, pp. 84–86.
8. Christie Su, "Lee Maps 6-Point Policy for Taiwan-Mainland Relations," *Free China Journal* 12–13 (April 14, 1995): 1.
9. Li Ta-wei and Ch'iu Yuan-pin, "Min-i sui-juh liu-shui," p. 21.
10. This writer recommends that the ROC's leaders adopt a low profile for the next two to three years to achieve more "international space." For example, the ROC should try to enter United Nation organizations and build support from many countries before requesting the U.S. and Japan to support its entry into the U.N. General Assembly.

CHAPTER 3

Greater China and American Security

DAVID M. LAMPTON

A fascinating study by Ellsworth Carlson recounts the young Herbert Hoover's early involvement in North China at the Kailuan (or Kaiping) Mines as a mining engineer. That venture was undertaken in another period of Western economic enthusiasm for the potentialities of China. That mining venture, as I recall, ended in mutual recrimination, lawsuits, and litigation—with the Chinese suing Hoover's employer in a European court. I conclude from that experience that Sino-American relations are often a combustible mixture born of Chinese and Western enthusiasms that reality frequently cannot sustain. Mutual disappointment, recrimination, and conflict can be the explosive result. Perhaps we are again in an analogous period.

To address the greater China security issues, I will draw on a number of sources and experiences, most recent of which is a trip (and subsequent report) in May and June 1994 that I took with former Secretary of Defense Robert McNamara, former Vice Chairman of the Joint Chiefs of Staff David Jeremiah, and three other four-star officers to the People's Republic of China (PRC), Hong Kong, and Taiwan to look at military developments in the region. I would like to consider four questions: (1) What does "greater China" (the PRC, Taiwan, and Hong Kong, for these purposes) mean for regional and U.S. security? (2) What challenges does the PRC present to the United States? (3) How does the PRC view the United States in the security area? (4) What are the implications of all this for future U.S. policy?

What Does "Greater China" Mean for Security?

I start from the premise that the increasing economic interdependence of the PRC, Hong Kong, and Taiwan, considered alone as a single factor, is conducive to greater security in the East Asian region and this process promotes U.S. security interests. I believe this because economic interpenetration raises the potential costs of conflict for all involved parties and leads to the creation of constituencies in each society that will promote stability and seek to avoid catastrophic conflict. By the end of 1993, Taiwan had cumulatively invested (by conservative estimates) nearly $5 billion in the PRC and there was two-way trade between China's mainland and Taiwan in 1993 of $14–15 billion or more. The PRC is the largest "external" investor in Hong Kong (perhaps $20 billion), and Hong Kong is the single largest external investor in the PRC. In short, the economic costs of conflict among the three have grown enormously over the last fifteen years. Considered alone, I believe that this reduces the likelihood of severe conflict.

Not only has economic interdependence reduced the chances of severe conflict in the region, but the cultural and interpersonal exchanges that are occurring have reduced the chances of miscalculation by the PRC and Taiwan. There have been literally millions of visits from Taiwan to the PRC since 1987. Although the flow of PRC citizens to Taiwan has been much smaller (in the tens of thousands), it has been significant. And the exchanges are not just among ordinary citizens; political and bureaucratic influentials have been involved in the last two years in particular. In November 1994 John Chang was in Beijing for personal reasons; one of the members of PRC's Association for Relations Across the Taiwan Strait, Tang Shubei, went to Taiwan not long ago; and the Koo-Wang meeting in Singapore of April 1993 was a landmark.

Of course, economic rationality and better mutual understanding do not alone determine state policy, or assure peace, anywhere. Rising nationalism, conflicting interests, regional arms competition, and loss of internal control in any one of the three societies could produce conflict, even with mutual understanding and despite the economic costs. Having said this, however, I believe that increasing economic interdependence and cultural interaction among the PRC, Taiwan, and Hong Kong are profoundly important and in the U.S. interest. We should encourage this trend. Let me hasten to say, however, that I do not believe that increasing economic interdependence will necessarily (or even probably) lead to the political integration of the PRC and Taiwan. That development, it seems to me, is highly problematic.

PRC Challenges to U.S. Policy

First, either through the success of its current development effort or through its failure (and all the disruption that failure would imply), China will be one of the two or three dominant foreign policy issues for the United States for the remainder of this decade and well into the next century. Second, it should be our operative assumption that China will progressively modernize, that it will acquire more power and influence in the world, and that part of this increased influence will be in the form of gradually expanding military strength. Third, because of its historical experience, rising nationalism, and economic and other interests that occasionally collide with our own, China will not be easy to deal with from the U.S. perspective. Likewise, Beijing will find Washington difficult to deal with from time to time. And, finally, the United States must seize the window of opportunity provided by the next decade of China's rise to work with Beijing to assure that China is productively and appropriately involved in regional and global economic and security structures.

Failure to achieve such integration would be analogous to the earlier tragic failures peacefully and constructively to accommodate the rise of Germany and Japan. Let me emphasize, I am *not* asserting that China is embarked on a path remotely similar to that followed by Germany and Japan. I am saying, however, that the international system has never found it easy to adjust to major new actors and that China's size and pace of growth all are historically unprecedented. The global system must do a better job in mutual accommodation this time around; the United States has a major responsibility in this regard, as does the PRC.

China's emergence as a great power has to be seen against the background of two global macrotrends: rapid economic growth in much of the developing world and increased nationalism in the world today. With respect to global growth trends, the World Bank tells us that in 1990 "rich industrial countries" accounted for 55 percent of global economic output, while "developing" countries accounted for 44 percent. By the year 2020, it is estimated that the industrial countries' share will have dropped to 37 percent of global output and that the "developing" nations' percentage will have risen to 63 percent. Put another way, over the next quarter century, the industrial countries can expect an average annual economic growth of 2.7 percent, while the developing nations may move ahead at 5 percent.

Turning to China, the World Bank, Bill Overholt, and even conservative Japanese economic analysts tell us that China almost certainly will do better than the developing world average, probably far better. Reasons for this expectation are many but include: China's economic growth since 1980 averaging 8.6 percent, despite significant fluctuations in economic performance during that period; China's population having a high level of basic education and saving 37 percent of the gross domestic product; foreign direct investment (FDI) flooding into the PRC, amounting to US$26 billion in 1993 and US$29 billion in the first three-quarters of this year alone.[1] The overseas Chinese not only have provided huge amounts of capital to fuel growth but have brought management techniques and marketing networks to the mainland as well, and China has sought knowledge in the West, with about forty-five thousand students currently in the United States. According to Undersecretary of the Treasury Larry Summers, that is more students than the Soviet Union and Russia have sent to the United States during the entire period since the end of World War II. In short, while prudent analysts must expect wide swings in economic performance and some turmoil along the way on China's mainland, prudence also requires that one predict good economic performance over the long haul there.

Of course, there is another scenario, one that assumes that China may be unable to sustain economic growth and maintain political cohesion. Were the nontrivial possibility of this scenario to materialize, analysts would point to the current problems that foretold such developments. Inflation in China's cities is serious, and Beijing has yet to show that it can meet its money supply growth targets or gently contain its overheated capital investment. There is an obvious incongruity between its annual gross national product growth of 13 percent and its 2 percent annual expansion in transport and energy—China now has joined the ranks of net oil importers. Equally worrisome is the fiscal deficit run every year since 1980 (except 1985), and the budget still hemorrhages from the subsidies provided to ailing state enterprises. We also must not forget the political succession, unemployment, rising economic inequalities, a lack of civil institutions to help cope with mounting social pluralism, and a social safety net that has widening holes. In short, the problems are legion and the Chinese are justifiably worried. At the National People's Congress meeting in March 1994, deputies said:

> There are strained relations between cadres and the masses, as well as the outstanding problems of intensifying contradictions among the people. . . . It is necessary to pay attention to these problems and deal with them properly, otherwise social unrest and instability will ensue.

Failures or setbacks could also occur as a result of external difficulties. Conflict in Asia (or elsewhere) that involved China could have severe repercussions. It is unsurprising that Chinese leaders have a mantra about the importance of a peaceful international environment for their own economic plans.

Were the failure scenario to materialize, it would have regional and global effects. Among them would be accelerated migration, a more assertive and nationalistic foreign policy, an inability of China's political center to control the behavior of local authorities and local populations; the staggering human toll would be measured in huge losses of life and the lost opportunities of countless multitudes. Whatever one judges to be the odds of this scenario, it is in the interest of the United States and others to work with China to avoid that possibility.

In short, Americans should assume that China will succeed; that China will thereby become increasingly important; that we should do

what we can (with Beijing's cooperation) to smooth China's way to full
and equal participation in the global community; and that China's success is to be greatly preferred over its failure.

How Does the PRC See the United States in the Security Realm?

Rising nationalism is the second global macrotrend to which I referred
above. We see rising nationalism and micronationalism in the former
Yugoslavia, in many areas of the former Soviet Union, in regions of
central Europe, and in several parts of East and Southeast Asia. During
mid-November 1994 in the Philippines we saw further indications of
rising nationalistic, anti-American sentiment. In the United States, the
recent elections provide some indication that Americans, too, many be
influenced by nationalistic currents of their own.

A recent survey in Taiwan reported as follows: "Although 52 percent believe America is Taiwan's most important international partner,
only 22.4 percent said they like Uncle Sam." In his widely quoted con-
fidential memorandum to Secretary of State Christopher of last spring,
Assistant Secretary Winston Lord said:

> A series of American measures, threatened or employed, risk corrod-
> ing our positive image in the region, giving ammunition to those
> charging we are an international nanny, if not bully.

To the extent that such views are widespread or grow in magnitude
and frequency is a matter for serious concern. Such sentiments would
reduce cooperation between the United States and its friends in the
Asia-Pacific area, and this, in turn, would further reduce the willingness of Americans to sustain the kind of multifaceted presence so
important to long-term stability, and our economic success, in this
region.

Turning to China, nationalism is in evidence there as well. Chinese
scholars, some of whom are themselves liberal in political and social
outlook, are talking about nationalistic trends in the PRC today. China

has the best chance to become a strong and prosperous nation that it has enjoyed in several hundred years; Chinese across the political spectrum justifiably savor this prospect. How the PRC will deal with others as its power increases and how it may seek to redress perceived past injustices remain to be seen. But I believe that we are witnessing the second time that the Chinese people have "stood up" in the last forty-six years. In 1949 Chairman Mao Zedong made this declaration at Tiananmen, signifying China's full independence after a "century of humiliation" and civil war. Today, the Chinese are "standing up" again by making their full claims on the global system as a great nation. It is important, therefore, to understand how China's leaders see the outside world, how they view the United States, and how they will use their growing power.

Within China's diplomatic and military leadership, there are diverse views. Despite this diversity, however, there are some commonly expressed views as well. Some of these views open avenues for cooperation and others require better mutual understanding. The widely articulated views among diplomats in China are the following: (1) A big-power, global conflict is unlikely in the next two decades or so, and Asia is more tranquil than much of the rest of the world. (2) Economic development is the basis for comprehensive national power, and the economic realm is where one will see the bulk of competition and friction. (3) The comparative strength of the United States is declining relative to others in the region; the United States is overextended and has natural frictions in its relations with Japan and Russia, among others. (4) The United States, therefore, will be driven to cooperate with China. This imperative will, in turn, force Washington to moderate its objectives regarding internal change in China. (5) Internal politics will drive U.S. foreign policy in the final analysis. The jobs and economic well-being of Americans will prevail over value objectives in Washington. No U.S. leader, so this analysis goes, can long ignore China's economic potential and leave that growing market to the tender economic mercies of competitors in Japan, Europe, and this region.

Turning to the views of Chinese leaders in the national security realm, we find the following: (1) China will gradually and deliberately modernize its military over the next two decades. For the next decade or more such upgrading will be subordinate to economic modernization. Without a modern economic and technological base, it is infeasible to possess and sustain a modern military; a premature drive to achieve thoroughgoing military modernization would set back both economic development and military modernization itself. Nonetheless, China will have a modern military in the more distant future. China's senior leadership is quite candid about this. (2) There is a widespread feeling in the PRC that those abroad who now are talking about the "China threat" simply seek to keep the PRC in a subordinate position or sow discord between Beijing and its neighbors. As one Chinese general remarked to me in connection with outside analysts who talk about the China threat, "Why do they keep saying this? Do they want to keep China from becoming powerful?" (3) Consistent with the economic modernization priority, the Chinese military is selectively modernizing units, with an emphasis on air and naval capability. Such selective unit modernization is for the declared purpose of border defense, local conflicts, and making Beijing's claims in the South China Sea credible. (4) With respect to regional security discussions, there is a desire to keep them as informal as possible, there is a preference for bilateral (as opposed to multilateral) security *consultations*, and, as a matter of articulated policy, China is unwilling to concede that U.S. military forces in the region are a stabilizing influence. (Privately, some Chinese officials seem a bit more flexible on this point.)

Policy Implications for the United States

What does all this add up to in terms of how Americans might look at future policy toward the PRC and security issues in greater China? Most fundamentally, this combination of rising Chinese power and influence and increasing nationalism means that we must be exceedingly careful in managing bilateral relations with Beijing. The following thoughts might well guide us as we seek to manage this relationship.

First, China will be a major power, initially having regional capabilities and later acquiring global influence. The process by which this occurs will be gradual over the next two decades, and the character of this influence (and how it is exercised) will, in part, depend on the environment China faces now and in the period over which this development occurs.

Second, it therefore is important that we work together with China to develop a regional environment that is constructive and nonthreatening to everyone in the area. The entire outside world should encourage ever-greater degrees of transparency by Beijing in areas of decision making, military doctrine, and weapons procurement. Our common objective should be a consultative set of relationships in which force levels in the region are at the lowest possible stable level. For the foreseeable future, a continued, significant U.S. forward military presence in East Asia will be an indispensable element if stability is to be maintained.

We have a window of opportunity of perhaps a decade or two in which to build confidence, bilateral relations, and integrative regional and global regimes. We stand on the threshold of an era somewhat like that confronting post–World War II leaders in Europe who wisely embraced Germany in the postwar economic and security structures. We need to show similar vision today in thinking about China's participation in international regimes such as the General Agreement on Tariffs and Trade (GATT) and "full accession" to the Missile Technology Control Regime, for example. Parenthetically, I believe that China will soon enter GATT as a charter member of the World Trade Organization, though China still has much to do to bring its trading and economic system into sufficient conformity with GATT rules to win the approval not only of the United States but of China's European trading partners as well. By the same token, the United States must keep its markets open. Protectionism here would reduce U.S. leverage, slow global growth, and foster conflict throughout Asia.

Third, in addition to facilitating China's appropriate entry into the structure of regional and global regimes, we also need to create a stable, cooperative, and consultative relationship between China, Japan, Russia, and the United States. Any attempt to develop a regional "strategic triangle" or "quadrangle" in which there is an odd man out would be profoundly destabilizing. For the moment, a consultative and cooperative U.S.-China-Japan relationship is particularly important to the region. I believe, therefore, that it is highly desirable for Washington, Beijing, Tokyo, and Moscow to engage in regular, formal consultations among themselves, in addition to the many other multilateral and bilateral meetings that already occur. The fundamental stability of East Asia will depend on cooperation among the four major powers that intersect there. Finally, a sanctions-based, punitive approach to the Chinese, and indeed people throughout Asia, will generally fail because our competitors will not follow such a lead, and because it will feed the more destructive forms of nationalism in China and within the region. The United States must find ways vigorously and effectively to promote its interests without excessive reliance on publicly applied threats, unilateral sanctions, and lectures on morality.

Given China's emergence as a global power, it is important that we seize this window of opportunity. The responsibility, however, is not Washington's alone—Beijing must also show that the policy of engagement and cooperation can provide benefits for both sides and for the broader world community.

Note

1. It is unlikely that the growth rate of foreign direct investment into the PRC will be sustained at its current high level.

CHAPTER 4

U.S.-China
Economic Relations

NICHOLAS R. LARDY

China's emergence as a major world economic power poses far-reaching questions for the world economic system and for the United States in particular. Since its economic reforms began in the late 1970s, China has been among the world's fastest-growing economies. Real gross national product has expanded by more than 9 percent per annum, meaning that real output has more than quadrupled since 1978.

This stellar economic growth has been accompanied and in certain respects caused by an even more rapid expansion of foreign trade and inward foreign investment. By 1993 China's exports exceeded US$90 billion, accounting for 2.5 percent of world exports, more than four times its share on the eve of reform in 1977.[1] In the first eight months of 1994, China's exports grew by an astounding additional 31.5 percent compared with the same months of 1993, assuring that 1994 will mark another substantial increase in China's share of world exports.[2]

Foreign direct investment inflows to China reached almost US$26 billion in 1993, accounting for fully a third of all foreign direct investment flowing to developing countries.[3] Only the United States attracted more foreign investment than China. In the first nine months of 1994, foreign direct investment inflows increased by 49 percent compared with the first half of 1993, suggesting that China in 1994 will remain far and away the largest developing country recipient of foreign direct investment and may even surpass the United States as the most important single destination for foreign direct investment.[4] In addition to attracting unprecedented amounts of foreign direct investment, China has borrowed internationally on both concessional and commercial terms; has become a significant seller of bonds on international markets; and has raised additional investment funds through the sale of equities to foreigners on both domestic and international markets.

While these trends testify to China's considerable success in penetrating world markets for goods and capital, there is a darker side as well. Investment and commercial banks in the United States, Japan, and Europe have charged several state-owned entities with failing to meet their credit obligations. China has also emerged as the world's largest violator of intellectual property rights, producing prodigious quantities of pirated software, videotapes, compact discs, and books. U.S. losses alone were estimated to be more than US$800 million in 1993.[5] China's eight-year quest to become a participant in the General Agreement on Tariffs and Trade/World Trade Organization (GATT/WTO) has yet to be concluded, largely because China's major trading partners seek further reforms of China's economic and trade system that would make it more congruent with the expectations of the GATT/WTO. Foremost among these expected changes are reduced tariff and nontariff trade barriers, a more uniform trade regime, the elimination of foreign exchange restrictions on payments and transfers in connection with trade in goods and services, and the increased transparency of trade decision making. In the United States many have pointed to China's large and growing surplus in its trade with the United States (discussed further below) as evidence of the closed character of the Chinese market.

China's challenge to the world economic system is unique and stems from several factors. First, world financial and trade institutions, notably the GATT/WTO, are structured for market economies. The World Trade Organization to date has found it difficult to accept an economy that is neither a developed nor a developing economy, the two major variants of market economies recognized in the GATT charter. Yet China today, although its role in the international economy exceeds that of any other transition economy, is only partly a market economy.

Second, China combines, to an unprecedented degree, large absolute economic size with a relatively low level of per capita income. Indeed, in the postwar period, no other country with a per capita income as low as China's has played such an important absolute role in the world's trading and financial system.

Finally, China is the only country combining a global trade deficit with a large bilateral surplus in its trade with the United States. The bilateral U.S. deficit has been a major source of economic friction between China and the United States. However, U.S. policy toward China is all too frequently formulated as if China were, like Japan, a large global surplus country. As documented below, China remains on average a global trade deficit country, meaning that measures applied to Japan may be less relevant for it.

China as a Transition Economy

At the heart of the dispute between China, on the one hand, and the United States and other major participants in the Working Party to examine China's participation in the GATT/WTO, on the other, is China's insistence to date that it be treated as a developing country. Under the GATT/WTO, countries recognized as developing economies are automatically provided with "special and differential treatment," which gives them more time to come into compliance with the terms of the GATT/WTO. For example, developing countries have as long as eight years after accession to the GATT/WTO to phase out export subsidies, and there is no requirement to eliminate subsidies unless the country's exports of the product account for at least 3.5 percent of world exports of that product for two consecutive years. Nations acceding to the GATT/WTO as developed countries, by contrast, must adhere to the provisions of the subsidies code on entry.

The United States has taken the view that China is neither a developing nor a developed economy but rather a country in process of transition to a market-oriented economy. The United States seeks to deny China the maximum flexibility that would be automatically available if it were classified as a developing country but has said that the United States is "prepared to demonstrate the appropriate flexibility."[6]

The view that China should not qualify for automatic "special and differential treatment" is based on the argument that this provision was intended to assist those countries that cannot export or that are sharply disadvantaged in export markets. Although China's per capita income is well within the GATT/WTO guidelines for a developing economy, it is an export powerhouse whose foreign trade expanded at an annual rate of 24 percent between 1985 and 1993.[7] Thus, the United States seeks to negotiate each item individually, presumably hoping to hold China at or close to standards expected of developed countries on some provisions of its protocol, while being willing to allow a transition period approaching the length of time automatically extended to developing countries on other provisions.

There is little doubt that the deadlock over this issue reflects the unique conditions outlined above. If China were a typical developing country with a modest trade volume, it likely would have become a contracting party to the GATT some years ago. But a low per capita income economy in transition that also has had substantial success in penetrating world markets poses special problems for the GATT/WTO.

Issues in Bilateral U.S.-China Trade

Sino-U.S. trade in recent years has been characterized by a host of problems: violations of U.S. intellectual property rights; restrictions on access to China's domestic market by U.S. firms; Chinese violations of the multifiber agreement governing the sale of imported textiles and garments in the U.S. market; and the failure of the Chinese to provide national treatment for U.S. firms that seek to provide banking, insurance, shipping, and other services in China. A review of each of these issues lies well beyond the scope of this paper. Interested readers are referred to the author's study *China in the World Economy*.

One issue, however, does warrant greater consideration—the growing bilateral deficit that the United States incurs in its trade with China. According to U.S. data, China has recorded a surplus in its trade with the United States in every year since 1983. Initially the U.S. deficit was small, but it expanded rapidly in the late 1980s; by 1991 the U.S. deficit with China was second to only that with Japan. By 1993 the bilateral deficit had increased to almost US$23 billion, and on the basis of trade flows in the first five months of 1994, one agency of the U.S. government projected that the imbalance would reach US$28 billion in 1994.[8]

In a sense, the growing bilateral deficit underlines each of the issues listed above because it is widely believed that the bottom line effect of each of those issues is to increase U.S. exports from China and reduce U.S. imports to China. I, however, believe that this line of analysis is fundamentally flawed for two reasons.

Most important, it is difficult to infer much about openness from a country's trade data. Certainly the state of the bilateral trade balance between two countries normally provides almost no evidence on the relative openness of the two economies to trade. Many countries routinely incur trade deficits with one subset of their trading partners while running surpluses with another subset of partners.

Second, even if the bilateral balance of trade between China and the United States did reflect the relative openness of the two economies, it is important to recognize that neither country's trade data accurately measure the bilateral flows. In particular, neither country counts as an export to the other the goods that are initially exported to Hong Kong and then reexported to either the United States or China. Because in recent years from two-thirds to three-quarters of all Chinese goods sold to the United States have first been exported to Hong Kong, Chinese customs data on bilateral trade are almost worthless, vastly understating the importance of the United States as a market for Chinese goods. Similarly, from one-fifth to one-fourth of all United States goods sold to China in recent years first were exported to Hong Kong and were not recorded as exports to China. Thus, United States trade data suffer from the same problem, although the magnitude of understatement of U.S. exports is proportionately much less.

It is possible, using Hong Kong data on reexports, which are also cross classified by country of origin, to adjust U.S. trade data to take into account U.S. goods initially sold to Hong Kong and then reexported to China. If the Hong Kong pipeline is then taken into account, the U.S. trade deficit with China would seem to be even greater. In fact, however, it would be smaller because the large flow of China exports to the United States via Hong Kong includes the gross margins of Hong Kong entrepreneurs. In 1994 they amounted to fully one-fourth the value of Chinese reexports from Hong Kong. Appropriate adjustments reduce the officially reported U.S. bilateral trade deficit by fully one-third in recent years.

A country's global trade balance, under normal conditions, is a somewhat better indicator of openness than any bilateral balance. On this measure it is difficult to classify China as a closed economy. In two out of three years since reform began in 1978, it has incurred an over-all deficit in its trade account.[9] In most of these years, it also incurred a deficit on a current account basis. This trade deficit is hardly surprising given the large inflow of foreign capital through various channels, notably the record inflows of foreign direct investment and the borrow-ing abroad that increased China's external debt from under a billion US$ in 1978 to more than US$83 billion by the end of 1993.[10]

In other words, these large inflows of foreign capital finance China's global trade deficit. They also have a direct effect on the bilat-eral balance of trade between China and the United States. As busi-nesspeople in Taiwan and, particularly, Hong Kong have moved their labor-intensive manufacturing operations to China, the garments, foot-wear, toys, and so forth that they formerly exported from Taiwan and Hong Kong are increasingly exported from China, and the trade deficits of these countries with the United States have fallen. Thus between 1987 and 1993, as the bilateral U.S. deficit in trade with China expand-ed by about US$20 billion, U.S. deficits with Hong Kong and Taiwan declined by US$5.1 billion and US$7.8 billion, respectively.

When all these factors are taken into account, it is clear that the U.S. trade deficit with the three countries together, or what some call greater China, is a problem. It grew by about one-fourth over a period of six years. Moreover, because the global merchandise trade deficit of the United States fell from US$152.1 in 1987 to US$115.7 in 1993, the share of the global U.S. trade deficit accounted for by greater China rose, from about 17 percent in 1987 to 28 percent in 1993.

Yet this problem should not be exaggerated. It is important to adjust the official U.S. data on bilateral trade flows. Because they fail to count U.S. goods reexported from Hong Kong to China and over-state the value of Chinese goods reexported to the United States from Hong Kong, U.S. data overstate the bilateral trade imbalance with

China by a factor of one-third. They also include exports from Hong Kong and Taiwanese firms that moved to China. More significant from an economic perspective, it appears difficult to classify China as a closed economy because it usually imports far more than it exports, financing the imbalance with foreign capital inflows, notably foreign direct investment and external borrowing. Moreover, the bilateral balance of trade between China and the United States, as discussed above, partly reflects China's openness to foreign direct investment.

Policy Implications

President Clinton's May 26, 1994, announcement that he would renew China's most favored nation (MFN) trading status with the United States and that future renewals would no longer be linked to human rights conditions in China eliminated what in recent years had been the most contentious economic issue in bilateral relations between the two countries. This decision, in part, reflects the importance of the bilateral economic relationship.

China is far more important to the United States than is indicated by its absorption in 1993 of only US$8.8 billion of U.S. produced goods, less than 2 percent of total U.S. exports. Three factors underlie this judgment.

First, as discussed above, data compiled by the United States Department of Commerce understate U.S. exports to China by approximately one-third. In 1993 U.S. goods first sold to Hong Kong and then reexported to China reached almost US$3 billion. Taking these reexports into account, China was the tenth-largest U.S. export market in 1993.

Second, and more important, since 1990 China has been far and away the fastest growing foreign market for U.S. goods. U.S. exports to markets in developing countries in recent years have grown about five times more rapidly than exports to developed countries, partly because of recessions in Japan and Europe. But the growth of U.S. exports to China has outstripped even the pace of growth of exports to developing countries as a group. For example, the cumulative expansion of U.S. exports to China over the three years 1991–1993 was more than twice as great as the growth of exports to Mexico, Taiwan, Singapore, or Hong Kong and several times the growth of exports to South Korea.

Third, for the rest of the 1990s China likely will be one of the largest sources in the world of increased demand for imports. The World Bank estimates that East Asia will contribute between 35 and 45 percent of incremental global imports over this period.[11] China alone, whose imports grew by almost US$25 billion in 1993, is emerging as the single largest source of trade growth in East Asia. From the beginning of 1994 through the year 2000, China is likely to import US$1 trillion in capital goods such as transportation, telecommunications, computing, and power generation equipment—all areas in which the United States has a relatively strong position in international markets.

While renewing MFN and delinking future renewals from human rights conditions in China have set the stage for improved bilateral economic relations, current policy could be even more successful in meeting the president's articulated goal of engaging China more fully. The United States, as the only world economic superpower, is central to the process of integrating China more fully into the world economy. Two steps seem particularly appropriate to achieve that goal.

First, the United States should lift the most important remaining economic sanctions that were imposed on China in 1989. The Trade Development Assistance (TDA) and Overseas Private Investment Corporation (OPIC) programs should be reinstated in China. TDA provides grants to U.S. firms to do feasibility studies on potential projects abroad with the expectation that the specifications for the projects will lead to export orders for machinery and equipment or other components supplied by U.S. firms. Before 1989 TDA allocated a larger share of its funds for feasibility studies in China than in any other country, and it was judged to be one of the more successful programs in increasing U.S. exports. OPIC provides investment guarantees for U.S. firms investing abroad. Both these programs were suspended in 1989 in the wake of the slaughter of Chinese students in Tiananmen, and these sanctions were continued by President Clinton when he announced his MFN decision in May 1994.

Yet these sanctions do little or nothing to advance human rights in China. They only restrict opportunities for U.S. firms to be involved in infrastructure projects in China and reduce the flow of U.S. foreign direct investment to China. European and Japanese firms have access to funds from comparable programs from their government, while U.S. firms are handicapped in their commercial interactions with China.

Second, the United States should use MFN and other trade policies as tools to encourage further reform of China's foreign trade system. Specifically, in order to accelerate the process leading to China's participation in the GATT/WTO, the United States should offer more economic incentives in exchange for maximal reductions of tariffs and nontariff barriers by the Chinese in the final package negotiated on China's participation in the GATT/WTO.

In particular, the United States should offer to apply the ten-year phaseout of the multifiber agreement, a key part of the agreement growing out of the Uruguay Round of GATT negotiations. The phaseout, which will eliminate all textile quotas over a ten-year period beginning in 1995, is important to China because textiles are its single largest export. Yet the United States, under the provisions of the Jackson-Vanik amendment, will invoke article 35 of the GATT agreement, the so-called nonapplication provision, meaning that the United States will not apply the GATT with respect to China. Thus, unless it is separately covered in a bilateral side agreement at the time China enters the GATT, China will not benefit from the phaseout of the multifiber agreement in the U.S. market.

In the absence of such a side agreement, it is almost certain that China's exports of garments and textiles to the United States would decline significantly. The reason is that quota agreements restricting exports from other suppliers will be phased out, potentially providing them with an opportunity to displace garments and textiles previously supplied by the Chinese. In short, given the importance of China's textile and apparel sales in the U.S. market, offering to apply the phaseout of the multifiber agreement with respect to China should be a significant incentive for the Chinese to grant the further concessions necessary to make their trade regime compatible the expectations of the working party negotiating China's participation in the GATT.

In addition, the United States should agree to provide China with permanent MFN status in the U.S. market as soon as it is evident that

China is in compliance with the protocol governing its participation in the GATT, as well as bilateral economic agreements with the United States on intellectual property, trade in textiles, prison labor, and so forth. This means that the executive branch would have to seek congressional approval for repeal of the Jackson-Vanik amendment as it applies to China.

Lacking some increase in economic incentives to undertake what will be painful adjustments to its own domestic economy, the Chinese government might even abandon its attempt to become a participant in the GATT/WTO. Should that happen, the influence of the United States over the future direction of internal economic developments in China would be reduced. It would be better to provide the incentives encouraging the Chinese concessions that would make China's entry into the major world trade body possible. Once in the organization China would be subject to continuing pressure to conform to GATT/WTO norms. This is far preferable to the failure of the accession process.

Notes

1. Except where otherwise noted, data in this paper are taken from Nicholas R. Lardy, *China in the World Economy* (Washington, D.C.: Institute for International Economics, 1994).
2. *Guoji shangbao* (International business), September 14, 1994, p. 1.
3. *Wall Street Journal*, August 31, 1994, p. A2.
4. *China Daily*, October 24, 1994, p. 1.
5. Office of the United States Trade Representative, *1994 National Trade Estimate Report on Foreign Trade Barriers* (Washington, D.C.: U.S. Government Printing Office, 1994), p. 51.
6. Ambassador Charlene Barshefsky, deputy United States trade representative for GATT Affairs, "Statement on Trade Policy toward China," House Ways and Means Subcommittee on Trade, July 28, 1994.
7. Ambassador Charlene Barshefsky, transcript of a Hong Kong press conference, July 23, 1994.
8. Central Intelligence Agency, *China's Economy in 1993 and 1994: The Search for a Soft Landing* (Washington, D.C.: Central Intelligence Agency, Directorate of Intelligence, 1994), p. 30.
9. Based on official Chinese trade data in which imports are valued at cost, insurance, and freight paid prices while exports are valued in terms of free on board prices.
10. *Guoji shangbao* (International business), July 28, 1994, p. 1.
11. Vinod Thomas and Tamar Manuelyan Atinc, "China: Assuming Its Role in Global Trading," paper presented at the International Symposium on China's Foreign Economic and Trade Strategies in the 1990s, Beijing, May 11–14, 1994.

CHAPTER 5

The Importance of Human Rights in U.S. Policy toward China

MERLE GOLDMAN

An indication of the effectiveness of even the implied use of economic pressure in U.S. policy toward China can be seen in what happened after President Clinton in May 1994 delinked renewal of most favored nation (MFN) status from China's actions on human rights. Despite having given in to the demands of the Chinese government and U.S. business for delinkage, America's huge deficit with China continues to grow and repression of Chinese dissidents has become harsher. The argument that delinkage would be good for U.S. business and ultimately good for democracy in China has not been borne out by the facts.

Wang Juntao and Chen Ziming, the two major political prisoners charged with provoking the events that led to the crackdown on the Tiananmen demonstrators on June 4, 1989, were released in order to win Clinton's decision on delinkage. Wang was exiled to the United States and rearrested in June 1995, and Chen, who refused to go to the United States, was put under house arrest. The release of others associated with the demonstrations of spring 1989 came to an abrupt end, and negotiations with the International Committee of the Red Cross to check on the health of political prisoners were broken off.

Even more ominous, the leaders of human rights groups in Shanghai and Beijing who sought to register their organizations officially with the Ministry of Civil Affairs were arrested and then sent to labor reform camps. In addition, workers and intellectuals seeking to establish independent labor unions to protest against unsafe, exploitative work conditions were arrested. Several were sentenced to fifteen to twenty years, longer sentences than the thirteen years meted out to Wang and Chen as the supposed leaders of the 1989 Tiananmen demonstrations. A number of Chinese and Hong Kong journalists reporting from China have been arrested and given long sentences for minor offenses. Pressure has been put on the international press not to cover these human rights abuses, either threatening deportation or not allowing others from the same news agency to report from China.

China's most famous political dissident, Wei Jingsheng, who had been given a fifteen-year sentence in 1979, was released in the fall of 1993, just six months short of his term, in order to further China's chance of getting the Olympics in the year 2000. He has been rearrested and has not been heard from since mid-1994. Wang Dan, one of the student leaders of the 1989 Tiananmen demonstrations who had also been released early in order to get the Olympic bid, has been continuously harassed by the Public Security Bureau since the delinkage of MFN, and in late 1994, several of the police following Wang threatened to kill him. He too was rearrested in 1995. There have been renewed crackdowns on Christians who refuse to accept the religious leaders imposed by the party. In addition, the party has been particularly zealous in ferreting out and arresting participants in churches that went underground during the Cultural Revolution (1966–1976) and has stepped up its harassment of religious worshipers in Tibet.

Human Rights in the Mao and Deng Eras

Nevertheless, it should be remembered that there is a qualitative difference between the human rights abuses of the Deng and Mao Zedong (1949–1976) eras. Whereas Mao attacked whole classes of people— such as the Western-oriented intellectuals in the 1957–1959 antirightists campaign and millions of bureaucrats as well as intellectuals during the Cultural Revolution, not to mention causing the death of more than thirty million peasants during the course of his utopian Great Leap

Forward (1958–1960)—the Deng repression of dissidents is directed against specific individuals, not against their families, friends, and the class to which they belong. Moreover, unlike the Mao era, when they were imprisoned, died in captivity, or were released only after Mao's death in September 1976, dissidents in the Deng era usually reemerge into public life after an interval or when they are released from prison.

Therefore, it is ironic, that except for a few scholars and émigrés, there was little criticism made of the massive human rights abuses during the Mao period. In the early 1970s, when the United States opened relations with China, the Cultural Revolution was still under way, and it did not end until Mao's death. Yet the United States was so anxious to enlist China on its side in the cold war with the Soviet Union that U.S. leaders as well as the press were willing to overlook Mao's brutal suppression of his countrymen. Only after the military crackdown on the Tiananmen demonstrators on June 4, recorded on international television, did U.S. leaders, the press, and the public become concerned about China's human rights abuses.

Effective Policies in Dealing with Human Rights

Although decidedly not of the magnitude or severity of Mao's nationwide repressions, the Deng regime's abuses of human rights continue. Until mid-1994, the annual review of China's MFN status had acted at least as a constraint on these abuses. Because China's leaders have been more responsive to economic pressure, it is unlikely that the threat of noneconomic sanctions will be as effective in restraining them. Nevertheless, there are a few noneconomic approaches that may at least limit a worsening of the human rights situation.

Unlike Mao, who neither cared what the outside world thought nor desired to become a part of that world, the Deng leadership very much wants to participate in the world community and not just in an economic way. Under Deng, China has gradually accepted some of the international community's norms of conduct. It subscribes to the U.N.

Universal Declaration on Human Rights. Nevertheless, like their Asian brethren, China's leaders emphasize the declaration's rights to economic development and national sovereignty and pay little attention to the declaration's stipulations on political and individual rights. They argue that while political and individual rights characterize Western civilization, those rights are alien to China's traditions. Therefore, they assert, criticism of China's human rights abuses is an unwarranted interference in China's internal affairs.

China's leaders, however, do not know their own traditions. True, their traditions do not have the concept of "rights" per se, but the Confucian tradition does include the idea that intellectuals and others should criticize oppressive or immoral officials, no matter what their station. It is also true that China did not begin to talk about political rights until the late nineteenth century and individual rights until the early twentieth century. By now, however, these concepts have informed China's political discourse for more than a century. China's leaders may not know or want to know about these concepts, but many in the bureaucracy, in urban centers, and even in the rural areas, as well as in the intellectual community, especially after the persecution of some 100 million people during the Cultural Revolution, now care about political and individual rights, which are also stipulated in China's constitution. Some protesters say it was precisely because they did not assert these rights that they could not stop Mao's destructive policies before he died. They point to the development of political and individual rights in Taiwan to demonstrate that such rights are not alien to China's traditions.

The Impact of the Move to the Market on Human Rights

Western and Chinese businesspeople as well as China's leaders insist that as China's markets, international trade, and middle class expand, these economic forces will in time lead China toward democracy and an end to human rights abuses. Although this is a persuasive argument, democracy does not necessarily evolve automatically with the expansion of the market, international trade, and a middle class, as witness Germany in the 1930s.

So far, there is little evidence that the development of these economic forces in China has improved the human rights situation. Nor is there any indication that China's interaction with U.S. businesspeople and capitalism has in any way nudged China toward democracy. Such interaction helped introduce business and property law but not civil law or rights. Since 1989, it has been possible to bring suit against party officials for unfair treatment, but so far few claimants have won their suits.

The fact that China's East Asian neighbors—Japan, South Korea, and Taiwan—have gradually moved in a democratic direction does not mean China necessarily will. Moreover, we saw that Japan's move to the market and involvement in the international economy without comparable democratization in the early decades of the twentieth century was one of the factors leading it into World War II. It would not be to our advantage to see China follow Japan's historic pattern. In addition, China is much larger than South Korea and Taiwan and much less literate. It also has had a less egalitarian form of economic development. And unlike those countries, few of its political and business leaders have been trained in the West.

If we want to see China move in a democratic direction, we cannot just hope that economic forces will take it there. Without individuals committed to correcting human rights abuses and seeking to establish democratic institutions, there is no guarantee that China's move to the market will lead to democracy. It can be argued that it takes time for market forces to further the emergence of a democratic system. But until those forces work themselves out, what can be done to prevent those committed to democracy and human rights in China from being silenced or imprisoned? What can be done in the meantime to keep their views alive and their voices heard?

What Can Be Done?

The role of any foreigner in China's affairs, whether on the scene or from afar, is at best marginal. Nevertheless, there are ways short of economic pressure in which we can help. At the news conference when he delinked MFN from human rights, President Clinton suggested creating a voluntary code of conduct for U.S. businesspeople in China. Such a code might call for minimal labor standards, such as prohibition against the use of child labor, unwillingness to use parts supplied by prison labor, and rejection of political surveillance and party committees in joint enterprises. But even if such a code could be agreed on, it would be difficult to get compliance to a Sullivan-like code of ethics as we did in South Africa. Unlike our South African counterparts, the people with whom we deal in China do not care about human rights. Moreover, our competitors in China—overseas Chinese, Taiwan, South Korea, Japan, and even West European countries—are willing to conduct business without such a code. It is highly unlikely that U.S. businesspeople would comply with such a code, if compliance meant losing out to the competition. Equally important, China does not respond to private negotiations on human rights issues, whether with businesspeople or diplomats. (Behind-the-scenes negotiations have proven to be minimally effective.)

China's leaders, however, do respond to censure of its human rights abuses when censure is sufficiently public. Mao did not care about international censure, but China in the Deng era is concerned with its image in the world and wants to be accepted as a member of the establishment. Therefore, despite its qualified acceptance of the Universal Declaration on Human Rights, China is anxious to demonstrate that it is living up to this declaration. Its leaders have made human rights a major topic of study and set up relevant nongovernmental organizations (NGOs), headed by party officials, such as the Society for the Study of Human Rights, led by the former head of Xinhua. Even though the purpose of these efforts is to counter Western arguments, China's leaders today, unlike the Mao regime, are willing at least to engage in discussions on such issues.

Every year, China sends a large delegation to the U.N. Commission on Human Rights that meets in Geneva. In recent years, just before the meetings, which take place in February and March, China has released a number of well-known political prisoners or improved their prison conditions to show its good intentions. Its delegates do not even vote on most of the resolutions. Their major concern is to ensure that a resolution sponsored by the democratic countries criticizing China's human rights abuses does not pass and to demonstrate that China abides by the Universal Declaration. Thus, to engage China on human rights issues in a variety of public forums, particularly in international arenas, prods China into at least circumscribing its abuses so as to avoid public censure.

Another proposal that President Clinton had planned to make at his press conference was the establishment of a joint U.S.-China Committee on Human Rights, but Jimmy Carter, who was asked to head it, refused because he believed it would have been a sham. Indeed, it would be a sham, but in the Deng period a sham sometimes takes on substance. In Mao's China, for example, the National People's Congress was merely a rubber-stamp meeting, but under Deng, for the first time, it has become a public forum in which dissent from party policies is openly expressed. The U.S. Congress in 1994 had considered setting up such a joint committee with the National People's Congress. Their effort should be encouraged. American NGOs should also engage in dialogue with China's NGOs, even though they too are shams. But in the freer atmosphere of the Deng era, they also may take on substance. Finally, it is most important for individual Westerners to speak out on human rights issues in China because, even though the present leadership may not agree with the Western view, many Chinese with whom we deal do agree with the Western view. Several of them have privately thanked me for bringing up the issue publicly, something they cannot do and hold onto their jobs.

We should, therefore, continue to demand that China fulfill its promises to open its markets to U.S. goods and stop its infringement on U.S. property rights. It is equally and perhaps even more important, however, to speak out loudly and repeatedly about China's human rights abuses. If we do not, the few voices calling for democracy in

China today may be completely silenced. Certainly, a country the size of China with the power it has in Asia, if not the world, and one of the few that is presently increasing the percentage of its GNP going into the military, is one we want to see move in a democratic direction. If it does not, there may not be much peace or democracy in the next century.

CHAPTER 6

The U.S. Quest for Morality in Foreign Policy and the Issue of Chinese Democratization

THOMAS A. METZGER

Chinese Democratization and the Principles of U.S. Foreign Policy

As described in the introduction above, U.S. leaders dealing with greater China face a variety of new policy problems. They cannot, however, deal with them by just following a straightforward calculus of realpolitik, trying maximally to ensure peace, promote international prosperity, and otherwise pursue U.S. interests. Our country, as George F. Kennan complained, remains influenced by a national vision demanding that U.S. foreign policy morally pursue the well-being of other nations.[1] Thus U.S. idealism has raised the philosophically and methodologically complex question of how to figure out what constitutes the well-being of a culturally exotic people. Precisely because of this idealism, U.S. policy toward China has long been and will long continue to be concerned with the problem of Chinese democratization.

Chinese democratization has two main aspects (leaving aside the question of Hong Kong).[2] The first is the democratization of the Republic of China (ROC), going back to liberalization in the late 1970s and reforms beginning in 1986. This process will be completed in 1996, when a free election will decide who is to be president.[3] The second aspect consists of the many ways in which various mainland or mainland-linked Chinese circles after Mao's death in 1976 used the ideal of democracy to denounce the current government of the People's Republic of China (PRC) as tyrannical or at least to criticize it. The basic facts about this amorphous movement are well-known. As already noted, Teng Hsiao-p'ing's reforms since 1978 have created a remarkably successful "socialist market economy," even though the relative prosperity of 100 to 200 million Chinese on the mainland depends on the docility of some 900 million Chinese who have remained thoroughly and desperately mired in extreme poverty. But Teng combined these economic reforms with an insistence on the continuing dictatorship of the Chinese Communist Party (the "Four Cardinal Principles"). This insistence outraged many Chinese, especially intellectuals. Moreover, the extent on the mainland of the popular demand for democracy probably increased in the 1980s. True, many if not the vast majority of the Chinese, especially in the 1990s, have been either unaware of these Chinese demands for democracy, uninterested in them, ambivalent about them, or critical of them as impractical and irresponsible. As always, one must take into account what Min Hung-k'uei called "the silent majority," rural or urban Chinese traditionally focusing on their own careers and the well-being of their families rather than political issues, such as the "petty bourgeoisie" (*hsiao-shih-min*) and the many students, professors, and other professionals who have typically shunned political demonstrations.[4] Moreover, often enough, the dissidents themselves intensely competed for public attention with one another and viewed each other as self-seeking and intellectually confused.[5] Nevertheless, somewhat as in the case of Taiwan during the 1970s and 1980s, Chinese voices calling for democracy on the mainland have a major effect on public opinion throughout much of the world, especially U.S. academic and political circles, and undoubtedly constitute a domestic as well as an international force with which the PRC leaders have to reckon.

After the arrest of one of the prodemocracy dissidents (Wei Ching-sheng) in 1979, the tension between dissident circles and the government gradually increased. During the 1980s, notably at Beijing University and Beijing's Chinese Academy of Social Sciences, a complex, extremely intense public discussion arose asking why Chinese history in the last seventy years had failed to realize the May Fourth ideal of democracy and to what extent this ideal was out of accord with China's inherited culture. The overseas scholar Ku Hsin has analyzed the extremely blurred spectrum of positions developed in the course of this discussion, ranging from Marxist views close to the party line, more humanistic Marxism, standpoints focusing on the Confucian tradition, and explicitly anti-Marxist views to the ideas of a few overseas Chinese influential on the mainland, especially Lin Yü-sheng of the University of Wisconsin and Tu Wei-ming of Harvard University.[6] Closely linked to this intellectual discussion, various student protest movements arose, culminating in the massacre of students in Beijing on June 4, 1989. After this, many dissidents went overseas, and nearly all of them in China ceased overtly challenging the government.[7]

Clearly, given the historical moral component in U.S. foreign policy, there is no question that the United States, within the limits of a prudent concern with its own interests, should support the ROC as a promising newcomer to the world of democratic polities. The morally puzzling problem is the extent to which the United States should support Chinese circles demanding democracy for the mainland, as opposed to working with the PRC leaders to further political stability and the rise of the market economy there.[8]

A common view in U.S. human rights and Chinese dissident circles is that the Chinese demand for democracy is moral, that the PRC's refusal to democratize is immoral, and that therefore the moral component in U.S. foreign policy must translate into full support for the demands of the dissidents. From this standpoint, any attenuation of that support on the part of the United States can be based only on the prudent but selfish pursuit of national interests and so can be morally justified only if, in some libertarian or utilitarian way, such selfishness is identified with morality.[9]

This view, however, is simplistic and untenable. Attenuation of U.S. support for the prodemocracy dissidents can be justified in persuasively moral terms, not just by using the morally precarious language of prudence. The moral justification for such attenuation is clear when we look at the sociological study of the institutionalization of democracy; at the relation between democracy and the question of a nation's overall well-being; at the role of culture in determining how a nation can most rationally pursue its well-being; and at the tradition-rooted utopianism and even Marxism of the dissidents, which has so far prevented them from presenting a prudent, credible political program, one which could be practicably implemented as an alternative to the current system. It would be a great mistake to let U.S. foreign policy be captured by the groups identifying morality with a simplistic demand maximally to hasten the democratization of the mainland.

The Sociology of Democratization

If one looks at the ideas so far developed by social scientists and historians about "the social requisites of democracy," as summed up by Seymour Martin Lipset in his 1993 presidential address to the American Sociological Association,[10] it is clear that pressing for immediate democratization is not necessarily the most effective way to democratize in all cases and that, therefore, in some cases nondemocratic, authoritarian rule may be advisable during periods of transition during which the social requisites of democratization can be further realized. This point logically but paradoxically and unpleasantly implies that, in order effectively to further democratization, a government working to realize the social requisites of democracy may have to maintain political stability by forcibly restraining dissenters whose efforts to quicken democratization threaten instability. Lipset regards as possibly reasonable the suggestion that "*perestroika* (economic and social reform) *must precede glasnost* (political freedom)."[11]

This judgment is a possibly reasonable one because the causative relationships between the social requisites of democracy, as Lipset argues, do not follow any objective law of development calling for maximally speedy democratization. Instead of such an objective law, social scientists find only variables whose causal interrelationships cannot be confidently predicted. Says Lipset: "Given the multivariate nature of whatever causal nexus is suggested, it is inevitable that any given variable or policy will be associated with contradictory outcomes." Lipset's point echoes that of William Graham Sumner made about one hundred years ago: "We have, as yet, no calculus for the variable elements which enter into social problems and no analysis which can unravel their complications."[12] In other words, many policy decisions can be based only on controversial practical judgments, not on scientifically demonstrable principles. Moreover, instead of probabilistically indicating that speedy democratization usually leads to successful democratization, the data probabilistically indicate that successful, stable democratization is unlikely unless certain social requisites have first been realized. Although liberals in the ROC today often claim that the growing pains of this young democracy are so great because democratization was not carried out earlier, Lipset implies that, had it been carried out before economic modernization, urbanization, and the rise of a well-educated middle class occurred, Taiwan's democratization, instead of suffering growing pains, might well have failed. Both of these views are only probabilistic, but Lipset's is based on the empirical finding that democratization has often or always failed when unaccompanied by certain "social requisites."

According to his analysis, economic modernization (including the institutionalization of capitalism) is only one of these requisites. Avoiding the strict confines of rational choice theory, he emphasizes another one: the cultural or religious framework legitimizing what I would describe as "the three marketplaces." I here will use my own formulations to sum up what he says under the headings of "political culture," "religious tradition," and "legitimacy."[13]

The Hayekian idea of the "three marketplaces" refers to the freedom, broad though usually not absolute, of the individual to buy and sell as she prefers, to support or oppose political leaders as she prefers, and to affirm or reject ideas as she prefers. The accumulation of such individual choices forms the economic, political, and information or intellectual marketplaces. Such individual freedom is often affirmed by proponents of democracy, but the two great Western traditions of democratic thought, the Rousseau-Hegel-Marx tradition and the Locke–*Federalist Papers*–J. S. Mill tradition, differ on the extent to which individuals can be allowed freely to make unpredictable choices violating scientific and moral principles. As Charles E. Lindblom suggested, the Rousseau tradition has bred the optimistic belief that this unpleasant unpredictability can be minimized by identifying a moral-intellectual elite who can use political power to put rational limits on individual freedom, while the Millsian tradition lacks this optimism. It therefore prefers to minimize the limits on individual freedom, letting society risk suffering from the unpredictable consequences of the three marketplaces, even if silly ideas displace good ones, silly voters elect bad officials, and free enterprise leads to gross economic and political inequality as well as painful economic cycles.[14] The Millsian tradition has tried to minimize limits on individual freedom especially by reducing these parameters to formal rules of the game, differentiating these from the free competition between substantive moral and political claims—"the rule of law."[15]

The Millsian tradition, many would agree today, seems needed to effect economic modernization and democratization, but east and west there is a plethora of cultural traditions incompatible with it to varying degrees, including the Confucian tradition. The Rousseauistic tradition has been widely discredited, but, paradoxically enough, in many different cultural contexts, it is the Rousseauistic, not the Millsian, tradition that meshes most easily with common sense. Lipset notes that "historically, there have been negative relationships between democracy and Catholicism, Orthodox Christianity, Islam, and Confucianism; conversely Protestantism and democracy have been positively interlinked." Even apart from that "radicalization" of modern Chinese thought discussed by Yü Ying-shih, the Millsian tradition was largely rejected by Chinese in modern times, and Lipset adduces a similar resistance to it in Russia and Eastern Europe today. The Arab-Muslim case is too obvious for comment.[16] The process of legitimizing the Millsian tradition, which creates anxiety in many people by seemingly leaving society under the control not of wise leaders but of morally and intellectually ungraded, chaotic individual impulses, can be called "secularization," but secularization in many cultures is an exercise at least as precarious as economic development. Thus I would emphasize cultural development as a social requisite of democratization even more than Lipset does. As Samuel P. Huntington recently observed, deep differences between cultures persist today, and it is doubtful that they will be erased by those modern ways that have come to be so widely shared around the globe.[17] These differences are clearly important, even though many social scientists ignore them because they are so hard to study in a precise, quantitative way.

Besides economic modernization and cultural development, Lipset analyzes as a social requisite of democracy the rise of institutions that can challenge the state's monopoly over the distribution of wealth, power, and prestige, such as courts, elections, representative assemblies, political parties, and other kinds of groupings that can form a civil society mediating between the individual and the state and so helping peacefully to resolve conflicts of interest. As illustrated by Taiwan's long tradition of regular and lively local elections, going back to 1946, one year after the ROC took Taiwan back from the Japanese, the values articulated in the Millsian tradition, particularly political tolerance, can perhaps be formed even without the help of the philosophers by people simply doing what people in democracies do.[18]

Besides economic modernization, cultural development, and institutional growth, the social requisites of democracy, according to Lipset, include the great variety of ways in which the political demand for democracy arises. These include crisis situations, such as military defeats discrediting an authoritarian regime; the achievements of gifted political leaders ("pact building"); and the effects of powerful groupings or networks affirming the ideal of democracy, whether a social class, a colonial power, a system of military occupation, an international agency such as the World Bank, or a political party. Reinhard Bendix would add "intellectual mobilization," whether in the case of the West or that of "latecomer" societies using foreign societies as reference groups.[19] Lipset sees "the working class" as a major force, "particularly in the West," demanding democratization,[20] but the recent democratization of Taiwan was based far more on intellectual mobilization. Finally, Lipset discusses as a requisite of democracy the making of choices regarding formal political structure, such as choosing between the presidential and the parliamentary system or between different election procedures.

To use William Graham Sumner's distinction, domestic and international demands for democracy, choices about formal structure, and institution building are matters more of "enacted" change that can be hastened, while economic modernization and cultural development are more a matter of "crescive" changes not easily hastened. Exactly what can be hastened just when, however, is inherently a matter of controversial practical judgment, not one of doubt-free scientific demonstration. Therefore it is a question about which reasonable people can disagree, not one regarding which correctness and morality are necessarily on the side of those wanting maximally to speed up democratization.

Democratization and the Pursuit of National Well-Being

If the speed with which democratization should occur is a matter of probabilistic practical judgment, so is the question of the practical, causative relationship between democratization and other processes also vital to a society's well-being (*fu-li*), though this issue has been little discussed in recent times by U.S. scholars. The desire for democracy is widespread in the Chinese world, but Chinese since the late nineteenth century have seen their well-being as equally or even more contingent on their reaching the goal of *fu-ch'iang* (wealth and power), in other words, economic modernization and national security. Similarly, Franklin Delano Roosevelt's Four Freedoms, set forth on January 6, 1941, as the goal of the U.S. war effort, included "freedom from want" (economic development) and "freedom from fear" (national security). National well-being, in other words, is often viewed as a package deal.[21] Besides democratization, economic development, and national security, many emphasize what James Q. Wilson has recently called "the civilizing process" and "character," values close to the *lun-li* (ethics) commonly seen by Chinese as vital for societal well-being and to that concept of "civilization" so central to J. S. Mill's "On Liberty."[22] A fifth value has been much discussed in recent years: promoting ecological and other aspects of global well-being vital to national well-being. Moreover, whether democratization is the most important among these five goals is a matter of practical, philosophical judgment, not a question that can be scientifically settled. In other words, whether democratization should be slowed in order more effectively to pursue other national goals is a question about which reasonable people can disagree, not one regarding which rationality and morality are all on the side of those seeking maximally quick democratization. Let us not forget that John Stuart Mill himself, the father of modern liberalism, believed that democracy ("liberty") was suitable only for a prosperous, "civilized" society free of grave national security problems.

Culture and Political Reasoning

What few Chinese or Westerners will disagree about is that, in weighing all these probabilistic issues, priorities should be set on the basis of reason. *Li-hsing* (reason) is a word universally emphasized in all modern Chinese political writing, whether Marxist, Sunist, liberal, or New Confucian. But this consensus about the need for reason raises a basic philosophic question that has been discussed by philosophers such as Richard J. Bernstein and Ernest Geller and the political theorist John Dunn: Does "reason" refer to a kind of algorism, an objective, universal set of rules of successful thinking that overarch cultural boundaries and historically disparate situations and that everyone should respect? Or does it denote ways of distinguishing between sense and nonsense that vary inter- and intraculturally and cannot easily be subsumed under one standard of correctness?

The three eminent scholars above incline to the latter possibility. Thus while sociologists like Lipset see the problem of political causation and policy prioritization as probabilistic issues that cannot be resolved by appealing to a single, universal standard of correctness, prominent Western philosophers today similarly hold that culturally different perspectives on such probabilistic issues cannot be simply superseded by appealing to some one, transcultural, ahistorical standard of political rationality.[23] As many Asians have recently argued, then, Americans should not simply assume that their culturally parochial views about how to prioritize political goals and discuss political causation should necessarily override indigenous views elsewhere.

To say this is not to say that Americans putting the highest priority on the immediate democratization of China are *necessarily* wrong. For one thing, respect for the culturally distinctive views of the Chinese themselves would not of itself contradict this American view, since, quite obviously, there are many Chinese who themselves agree with this American sense of priorities. Yet even if no Chinese favored immediate democratization, Americans could still reasonably favor it, in the eyes of philosophers like Bernstein and Dunn. What such scholars reject is "objectivism," the belief that objective standards of political rationality can be established in a rigorously objective way similar, say, to biological or at least medical reasoning. What they still accept is the validity of argument, whether inter- or intracultural, as a collegial, albeit fallible way of determining "good reasons" to act one way or another. This collegial quest for "good reasons," therefore, should respect cultural perspectives as part of a practical problem, not treat such perspectives as absolute truths, not to mention simplistically reducing a complex intracultural problematic to a simple set of unambiguous values. Therefore, Westerners trying to make sense of the arguments within the Chinese cultural arena between those wanting to speed up and those wanting to slow down democratization can only describe these Chinese arguments and then themselves argue in favor of one or another of them, not *prove* that one Chinese argument or another is the only correct one. There is, in other words, no transcultural rational-moral standard according to which those Chinese wanting to speed up democratization are necessarily right. There is only a competition between culturally and otherwise biased ways of reasoning about political priorities and probabilities.

Prudence and the
Mainland's Democracy Movement

Entering this competition, I argue that the extent to which Americans should support the current Chinese movement demanding the quick democratization of the PRC depends on the extent to which this movement is working prudently to pursue the well-being of the Chinese people and not just propagating utopian ideals and criticizing the regime in a one-sided, self-serving way. To be sure, some persons favoring this movement in private conversation express prudent, sophisticated views. But the contribution a political movement can make depends to a considerable extent on the ideas it explicitly propagates to articulate its goals and unify itself. One has to know what these publicized ideas are before one can judge whether the current Chinese democracy movement is a prudent one reliably articulating the priorities needed to pursue the well-being of the Chinese people.

What are these ideas? Some widely circulated answers to this question are mistaken. Many scholars, even prominent ones, just accept this movement's self-image, seeing it as simply embracing the universally obvious principles of democracy and liberalism.[24] This prevalent notion is hard to refute because, east and west, people so commonly believe that these principles are indeed obvious. Actually, as already noted, this popular view is refuted by the virtually uncontroversial scholarly finding that Western thought about democracy has consisted of two very different political approaches, the Rousseaustic and the Millsian. It is also clear that the current Chinese democracy movement has based itself purely on the May Fourth tradition, which embraced the same Rousseauistic, entirely theoretical vision of democracy that Maoism grew out of.[25] Not surprisingly, therefore, this movement, as John K. Fairbank noted, has naively pursued sublime, utopian goals of political development.[26] Conversely, it has consistently refused to develop a democratization program not by espousing purely theoretical ideals but by taking into account the Taiwan experience as shedding light on the practical problems Chinese modernization and democratization entail.[27]

Its attitude toward the Taiwan experience is most significant. To be sure, whether a political attitude is rational, practical, and prudent is a matter of probabilistic judgment based on always debatable assumptions about the causes for economic-political success and about the level of success for which a political movement should aim. My opinion is that it is irrational for mainlanders to assume that the mainland can aim for a higher level of economic and political success than

Taiwan has already reached and to refuse seriously to consider using the cultural and institutional methods Taiwan used to reach it.

While this irrationality and utopianism are ignored by many writing about the mainland's democracy movement, many also mistakenly say that mainland intellectuals do not seriously believe in Marxism-Leninism and Maoism anymore. To begin with, as already indicated, political views today on the mainland and in overseas, mainland-linked circles form a highly blurred spectrum, not a clear dichotomy between the Marxist-Maoist party line and the democracy movement. This is clear from Ku Hsin's study,[28] but it is even clearer from reading the books put out by the scholars today most respected in Chinese intellectual circles outside the political center, such as Li Tse-hou (b. 1930). Li is an extremely gifted writer on modern Chinese intellectual history. There already is a considerable literature on him.[29] A 1992 article by Lin Min on him in the *China Quarterly* says that he is "one of China's most influential intellectuals," that his "contribution to what many regard as China's new enlightenment movement in post-Mao era cannot be overestimated," and that "Li's theories will continue to occupy the centre of the Chinese ideological stage, whether receiving official criticism or official sanction."[30] In 1987, a prominent Hong Kong publication called Li, Fang Li-chih, Chin Kuan-t'ao, and Wen Yuan-k'ai the four intellectual leaders of the Chinese youth.[31]

Lin Min grants that Li "does not reject the existing ideology completely," thus correctly recognizing Li's tendency to affirm Maoism. Lin, however, tries to argue that, in Li's thought, the emphasis is not on Marxism and Maoism but on "a gradual, continuous transition from the old discourse to the new," on an effort to make the "existing ideology . . . more open and dynamic."[32] Yet although Li is indeed seeking a fresh and more open kind of intellectual synthesis, the affirmation of Maoism in his thought is full and fervent, not an idea he is gradually discarding. Ku Hsin points out that at least through 1993, Li continued firmly to adhere to the Marxist ideas in his writings. In 1992, an overseas Chinese periodical called him "contemporary China's leading Marxist theorist on the question of culture."[33]

More to the point, his Marxism is not just a kind of humanism similar, say, to the thought of Ernst Bloch. To be sure, Li draws broadly from non-Marxist thinkers like Kant and Piaget to discuss ultimate philosophical or psychological questions, such as how to deal with the contradiction between materialism and idealism. Yet whatever the nature of his ultimate epistemological and ontological concepts—and these anyway include explicit, full acceptance of Marx's historical materialism—Li fervently endorses the basic thrust of Mao's thought and leadership. As Ku Hsin's thorough analysis shows, Li's basic philosophical position is that (1) Marx's materialism succeeds where Kant and Hegel failed in demonstrating the unity of subject and object; (2) this materialism entails a law of dialectical historical development; (3) people should use positive, revolutionary means to follow that law; (4) revolution includes sacrificing the individual to the social whole; (5) history follows the sequence feudalism-capitalism-socialism; (6) Mao successfully embodied the revolution leading out of feudalism but then mistakenly tried to realize socialism before the material base had sufficiently progressed.[34]

Thus Li's position does not basically differ from the official line that Mao's record was 70 percent good, 30 percent bad. Writing ten years after the Cultural Revolution, around 1986–1987, Li praised Mao as one of "the three greatest figures in the history of modern Chinese thought" and offered the following enthusiastic assessment of his life: "Confronting the individual's and and the nation's stormy, changing seas of life and death, relying on the 'impulses' coming from the power of his will to pursue great, far-reaching plans, on his own mental and physical resources, taking charge of the fate of the Chinese people—all this fully to realize the potential of his own body and spirit, to turn China into an ideal society, one based on the Great Oneness—such, more or less, was the unchanging worldview basic to Mao's actions from the time of his youth until his old age."[35] Logically integrating this assessment of Mao's historical role into his whole interpretation of the history of Chinese thought in three volumes,[36] Li depicts Mao as embracing a fundamentally correct theory of history (Marxism), brilliantly designing a revolution needed to free the poor from the oppressiveness of "feudalism," motivated by the moral side of Confucianism (its "practical reason"), working to turn "politics into morality . . . and law," and thus trying to realize a society in which the emphasis on

"instrumental rationality" will not lead to "cold, harsh monetary relations, extreme individualism, unbearably chaotic anarchism, and one-
sidedly mechanical rationality."[37] Given all these admirable qualities,
Mao in 1949 genuinely "liberated" the Chinese people, initiating an era
"filled with idealism and high hopes." For Li, Mao went wrong mainly in not understanding what Li says Marx and Stalin understood, that
political and social reforms must await the development of the material base. Trying to introduce socialism too quickly, in 1957, Mao
plunged the society into disaster.[38]

This continuing belief in Maoism now still so prevalent among the
elite, both outside and inside the political center, indicates that the
PRC's government is still legitimized. Many scholars believe that the
disaster of the Cultural Revolution delegitimized it. Yet legitimization
in Chinese history has often taken precisely this form of ambivalent
acceptance, with scholars outside the political center bitterly criticizing
the shortcomings of its ideology, policies, and personnel while simultaneously affirming its basic ideological premises. (This form of legit-
imation is part of what I have elsewhere tried to describe as an "inhibited political center.")

Thus basically in harmony with Teng's reforms and affirming the
democratic values of freedom and equality, Li easily appears in Western eyes as a thinker devoted to liberalism and pragmatism, but his
strong, persisting affirmation of Marxist theory and Mao's ideals dis-
tances him from a pragmatic, Millsian approach to modernization and
democratization, not to mention his estrangement from the practical
example of Taiwan's modernization and democratization. Moreover,
while many mainland intellectuals outside the political center are like
Li in explicitly endorsing Marxism, such as Liu Pin-yen, many who
claim to reject Marxism, such as the influential Chin Kuan-t'ao, can
best be seen as using Western and Taiwan scholarship to develop a still
basically Marxist view of China's history and prospects.[39] The overseas
scholar Ku Hsin has recently analyzed the whole spectrum of contemporary Chinese thought as still trapped in a Hegelian paradigm shared
by both orthodox Marxism and Confucianism.[40] True, there are other
ways of studying the shared premises of contemporary China's political discourse and the continuities between it and the Confucian tradi-

tion.[41] Yet Ku Hsin's analysis illuminates ideological problems that afflict the contemporary democracy movement, preventing it from criticizing the PRC in a balanced way and developing a practicable alternative to the current regime. A more sober, balanced approach to modernization and democratization in China can be found in the writings of the famous Hong Kong sociologist Chin Yao-chi (Ambrose Y. C. King), who fully appreciates the Taiwan experience, but his views are, unfortunately, well outside the mainstream of the mainland's democracy movement.[42]

To go back to the question, discussed above, of cultural secularization as a social requisite of democracy, one can say that the strongly Rousseauistic, utopian bent of the mainland's prodemocracy movement indicates that this requisite is still far from having been met there. The political demand for democracy has emerged there, albeit to a limited extent. Yet it has not taken that Millsian form that, many would argue, is needed to facilitate the practical institutionalization of democracy. The democracy movement there is part of the problem, at least as much as it is part of the solution, because, haughtily spurning the practical experience of Taiwan, it does not articulate practicable ways of gradually enhancing the overall well-being of the society.

Therefore, as Americans in their traditionally idealistic way seek a foreign policy that will morally promote China's well-being, not only U.S. interests, they cannot assume that the current Chinese demands to hasten democratization necessarily constitute the most moral and rational way to pursue that well-being. American and Chinese believers in democracy often appear to each other to be talking the same political language, but this is an illusion due to the difficulties of intercultural communication. In the world of economic-political development, morality cannot be separated from practicability. Good judgment about how to set political priorities requires prudence and pragmatism, not utopianism, and what seems prudent and rational in one cultural context may not in another. Americans will do well to take seriously those many Chinese—a vast majority, I would say—whose cultural predilections and view of political probabilities lead them to feel that the still very poor mainland so far lacks many of the social requisites of democracy and needs political stability in order to develop these. The current democracy movement's demand for a more democratic kind of political life on the mainland is one of the elements vitally needed to realize a better society there, but only one of them. The more this movement discards its utopian bent and addresses economic-political problems in a balanced, pragmatic way, the more will it contribute to the well-being of the Chinese people.

Notes

1. George F. Kennan, *American Diplomacy, 1900–1950* (Chicago: University of Chicago Press, 1951). For a recent expression of this traditional American demand for morality in foreign policy, see Robert N. Bellah et al., *The Good Society* (New York: Vintage Books, 1992), chap. 7.
2. On the Hong Kong situation compared with the ROC and PRC political structures, see Chin Yao-chi (Ambrose Y. C. King), *Chung-kuo-jen-te san-ko cheng-chih* (The Chinese people's three ways of government) (Taipei: Ching-chi yü sheng-huo ch'u-pan shih-yeh ku-fen yu-hsien kung-ssu, 1988).
3. See Ramon H. Myers, ed., *Two Societies in Opposition* (Stanford: Hoover Institution Press, 1991); Hung-mao Tien, *The Great Transition* (Stanford: Hoover Institution Press, 1989); and more recent articles by Myers and Ts'ai Ling.
4. For evidence of the large extent to which college professors and college students supported the KMT during the early 1980s, see Tien, *Great Transition*, p. 191. This Chinese use of "silent majority" is taken from Ku Ying, *I-ko hsiao-shih-min-te sheng-yin* (An ordinary citizen speaks out) (Taipei: Chung-yang jih-pao-she, 1972). Ku Ying is Min Hung-k'uei's pen name. My view of the mainland's "silent majority" is based on my own discussions with a considerable number of mainland Chinese and with my many Chinese friends.
5. See, for instance, the contemptuous account of Liu Hsiao-po's intellectual shallowness and concern with his own status within the democracy movement in Ku Hsin, *Chung-kuo fan-ch'uan-t'ung chu-i-te p'in-k'un— Liu Hsiao-po yü ou-hsiang-p'o-huai-te wu-t'o-pang* (The poverty of Chinese anti-traditionalism: Liu Hsiao-po and the iconoclastic utopia) (Taipei: Feng-yun shih-tai ch'u-pan kung-ssu, 1993). Liu Hsiao-po's harsh criticism of Li Tse-hou (or Ku Hsin's) is another example.

6. Ku Hsin, *Chung-kuo ch'i-meng-te li-shih t'u-ching* (The historical setting of the Chinese enlightenment) (Hong Kong: Oxford University Press, 1992).
7. A good deal of information about this development is in Merle Goldman, *Sowing the Seeds of Democracy* (Cambridge, Mass.: Harvard University Press, 1994).
8. For an argument favoring a fairly supportive U.S. policy toward the PRC, see Ramon H. Myers, *Thoughts on U.S. Foreign Policy toward the People's Republic of China*, Essays in Public Policy series (Stanford: Hoover Institution Press, 1994).
9. John Dunn seeks to emphasize "prudence" while rejecting utilitarianism. For him, "prudence" is an aspect of "practical reason." See, for example, his *Interpreting Political Responsibility* (Cambridge Eng.: Polity Press, 1990), p. 197. My argument could be rephrased to claim that if prudence is a virtue, not just a matter of enlightened self-interest, then it is moral to delay democratization in the PRC because quick democratization would be imprudent.
10. Seymour Martin Lipset, "The Social Requisites of Democracy Revisited: 1993 Presidential Address," *American Sociological Review* 59 (February 1994): 1–22.
11. Ibid., p. 17.
12. See ibid. and William Graham Sumner, "On the Mores," in Talcott Parsons et al., eds., *Theories of Society,* 2 vols. (Glencoe, Ill.: The Free Press of Glencoe, Inc., 1961), 2: 1043.
13. This notion of the "three marketplaces" is outlined in Thomas A. Metzger and Ramon H. Myers, "Introduction," and Metzger's "The Chinese Reconciliation of Moral-Sacred Values with Modern Pluralism," in Myers, ed., *Two Societies in Opposition.*
14. Charles E. Lindblom, *Politics and Markets* (New York: Basic Books, 1977), chap. 19. In distinguishing between these two Western intellectual traditions regarding the idea of democracy, I am making an uncontroversial point, so far as I know. In John Dunn, *Western Political Theory in the Face of the Future*, Canto edition (Cambridge, Eng.: Cambridge University Press, 1993), pp. 22–23, these two are referred to as the "strong" and the "weaker" versions of "democratic theory." This dichotomy also accords, I believe, with the analysis in David Held, *Models of Democracy* (Stanford: Stanford University Press, 1987).
15. See, for example, J. R. Lucas, "On Processes for Resolving Disputes," in Robert S. Summers, ed., *Essays in Legal Philosophy* (Berkeley: University of California Press, 1972), p. 180.
16. Lipset, "Presidential Address," pp. 1, 5. Yü Ying-shih's article is in

Daedalus 122, no. 2 (1993): 125–50. The Chinese failure to embrace Millsianism is discussed in Huang Ko-Wu, *I-ko pei-fang-ch'i-te hsuan-tse: Liang Ch'i-Ch'ao t'iao-shih ssu-hsiang-te yen-chiu* (The rejected path: A study of Liang Ch'i-ch'ao's accommodative thinking) (Taipei: Institute of Modern History, Academia Sinica, 1994).

17. Samuel P. Huntington, "The Clash of Civilizations?" *Foreign Affairs* 72, no. 3 (summer 1993): 22–49.

18. Professor Alex Inkeles has in conversation with me repeatedly emphasized this point.

19. Reinhard Bendix, *Kings or People* (Berkeley: University of California Press, 1978), pp. 265–72.

20. Lipset, "Presidential Address," p. 3.

21. For a discussion of the different values used to construct theories about human rights, see A. James Gregor and Maria Hsia Chang, *The Republic of China and U.S. Policy: A Study in Human Rights* (Washington, D.C.: Ethics and Public Policy Center, 1983), chap. 1.

22. James Q. Wilson, *On Character* (Washington, D.C.: AEI Press, 1991). For an attempt to discuss such criteria of national well-being, see *Issues & Studies* 23, no. 2 (February 1987), an issue devoted to the discussion of Chinese modernization and the methodology of evaluation, with articles by Alan P. L. Liu, Ramon H. Myers, and Thomas A. Metzger.

23. See John Dunn, *Political Obligation in its Historical Context* (Cambridge, Eng.: Cambridge University Press, 1980), chap. 10; Richard J. Bernstein, *Beyond Objectivism and Relativism* (Philadelphia: University of Pennsylvania Press, 1983); and Ernest Gellner, *Reason and Culture* (Oxford Eng.: Blackwell, 1992). In my *Contemporary China's Political Agenda and the Problem of Political Rationality: The 1994 Ch'ien Mu Lecture in History and Culture* (Hong Kong: Chinese University Press, in press), I try to describe a distinctive, mainstream, tradition-rooted Chinese way of defining political rationality, especially with regard to the questions of political goals, causation, and agency.

24. See, for example, Harvard professor Tu Wei-ming's views in *Tang-tai* 39 (July 1989): 72–74. I translate some of what he wrote there on p. 40 in the article by me cited in note 13 above.

25. See Huang Ko-Wu's book cited in note 16 above and other writings by him.

26. On this point, Fairbank quotes from one of my articles. See John K. Fairbank, *China: A New History* (Cambridge, Mass.: Harvard University Press, 1992), p. 424.

27. Liu Pin-yen's view of Taiwan is typical. It is adduced on p. 45 in the article of mine referred to in note 13 above. Disparagement of the

Taiwan experience is so common in the Chinese intellectual world on both sides of the strait that prominent Chinese scholars like Chin Yao-chi viewing it in strongly positive terms are exceptional. See my "The Sociological Imagination in China: Comments on the Thought of Chin Yao-chi (Ambrose Y. C. King)," *Journal of Asian Studies* 52, no. 4 (November 1993): 937–48.

28. Cited in note 16 above.

29. Much of it cited in Ku Hsin, *Hei-ko-erh-chu-i-te yu-ling yü Chung-kuo chih-shih fen-tzu: Li Tse-hou yen-chiu* (The dark spirit of Hegelianism and Chinese intellectuals: A study of the thought of Li Tse-hou) (Taipei: Feng-yun shih-tai ch'u-pan ku-fen yu-hsien kung-ssu, 1994). His high reputation in the West is reflected in the publication of Lin Min, "The Search for Modernity: Chinese Intellectual Discourse and Society, 1978–88—The Case of Li Zehou," *China Quarterly* 132 (December 1992): 969–98. A prominent panel at the 1993 annual meeting of the Association for Asian Studies was devoted to his work.

30. Lin Min, "The Search," pp. 972, 974.

31. Cited in Ku Hsin, *Hei-ko-erh*, p. 4.

32. Lin Min, "The Search," p. 971.

33. Ku Hsin, *Hei-ko-erh*, pp. 3, 9.

34. Ibid., chap. 4. By the 1990s, Li had started to move away from Maoism more, but the extent to which he has repudiated his admiration for Mao's life and thought is far from clear.

35. Li Tse-hou, *Chung-kuo hsien-tai ssu-hsiang shih-lun* (Essays on the history of Chinese thought since the 1911 revolution) (Taipei: Feng-yun shih-tai ch'u-pan kung-ssu, 1990), pp. 436–37, 175.

36. Besides the book cited in note 35 above, see his *Chung-kuo chin-tai ssu-hsiang shih-lun* (Essays on the history of Chinese thought in modern times) (Taipei: Feng-yun shih-tai ch'u-pan kung-ssu, 1990), also a powerful synthesis. Far more superficial but still important as part of his overall synthesis is his *Chung-kuo ku-tai ssu-hsiang shih-lun* (Essays on the history of Chinese thought in premodern times) (Taipei: Feng-yun shih-tai ch'u-pan kung-ssu, 1991).

37. Li, *Hsien-tai*, p. 426. This passage expresses Li's own ideal, which he implicitly identifies with Mao's goal of "the great oneness."

38. Ibid., pp. 222–33. On the continuing, widespread sense of identification in China today with Mao's ideals and revolutionary achievements, see Wang Gungwu, *The Chinese Way: China's Position in International Relations*, Norwegian Nobel Institute Lecture series (Stockholm: Scandinavia University Press, 1995).

39. See, for example, Chin Kuan-t'ao and Liu Ch'ing-feng, *K'ai-feng-*

chung-te pien-ch'ien: tsai lun Chung-kuo she-hui ch'ao-wen-ting chieh-kou (Modern China: Changes in the course of dealing with the modern intellectual world—another analysis of Chinese society's ultra-stable structure) (Hong Kong: Chinese University Press, 1993). I am currently preparing a critique of this extremely important, influential, and controversial book.

40. See his book cited in note 29 above.

41. See Huang K'o-Wu's review of the Ku Hsin book, which is cited in note 6 above. The review is in *Chin-tai Chung-kuo-shih yen-chiu t'ung-hsun* 17 (March 1994): 44–55. The problem of continuity between modern Chinese ideologies and the Confucian tradition is discussed in my forthcoming book cited in note 23 above; in my "Continuities between Modern and Premodern China," in Paul A. Cohen and Merle Goldman, eds., *Ideas Across Cultures* (Cambridge, Mass.: Council on East Asian Studies, Harvard University, 1990), pp. 263–92; and in my *What's Wrong with Chinese Thought? Essays on Modern Chinese Utopianism and its Traditional Roots* (forthcoming).

42. See my article on him cited in note 27 above.

CHAPTER 7

Concluding Reflections

Questions regarding the Idea of "Greater China"

GUO CHANGLIN

Frankly, I wonder whether the United States has a policy toward the so-called greater China. I would also argue with the notion or concept of greater China itself. Most of the international community recognizes that there is but one China and that Taiwan is part of China, Hong Kong is a part of China. So what most experts refer to as greater China today is actually China as it should be. China is great but is not greater.

For reasons you all know, China's unification remains a goal that has not yet been achieved. Hong Kong is still under British colonial control, and Taiwan, a legacy of World War II, remains separated from its motherland.

The normalization of diplomatic relations between China and Britain made the resolution of Hong Kong's return to China's sovereignty possible, and the normalization of relations between the United States and China also contributed to the relaxation of tension in the Taiwan Strait. But it was the end of the cold war as well as the rise of the economic factor in international relations that has really led to the growing interchange across the Taiwan Strait.

But the road toward China's unification has been bumpy, and the process has never been smooth. Externally, the government of the United States, while recognizing the government of the People's Republic of China as the "sole legal government" of China, also expressed interest in continuing "cultural, commercial, and other nonofficial relations" with Taiwan. Congress also passed the Taiwan Relations Act to provide a "legal rationale" or framework for the relationship. A decade after the Sino-British agreement on the normalization of relations, Britain suddenly raised the issue of democracy, thus threatening to stall cooperation between the two sides.

Internally, for the first time ever, debate within the Kuomintang about the "one-China" principle caught the attention of the world community and led to a drive to expand Taiwan's international living space. The Democratic Progressive Party is in a position to promote Taiwan's independence. This development in Taiwan made both the Chinese and the U.S. governments worry about its implications. This concern is broadly reflected in many policy papers sponsored by important think tanks and research institutes in the United States and has been expressed both publicly and privately by U.S. China scholars.

China is especially concerned about events in Taiwan. But it has not changed its fundamental policy of striving for the peaceful resolution of the Taiwan issue, although in principle it does not rule out the possibility of using force. But this is just in case, in cases that you know.

China's unification is reaching a critical period. We hope that the outside powers involved in the Taiwan issue, especially the United States, abide by the three communiqués with China and the three principles, especially the principle of one China, and refrain from contributing to the precarious and fragile situation in the Taiwan Strait.

U.S. Foreign Policy toward Greater China

LUNG-CHU CHEN

Overall, I think it would have been more appropriate to call this conference "U.S. Foreign Policy toward China, Hong Kong, and Taiwan" instead of "U.S. Foreign Policy and Greater China" because Taiwan is Taiwan, and China is China. Taiwan and China are two separate, sovereign states, diverging fundamentally in their political, economic, and social systems. Taiwan is *not* an internal affair of China. Taiwan is not part of greater China—legally, politically, or economically. Clearly, by China I mean the *PRC*, the People's Republic of China, not the *ROC*, the Republic of China.

The PRC's territorial claim to Taiwan, as most recently reiterated in its "Taiwan White Paper" of August 31, 1993, is as absurd as Iraq's territorial claim to Kuwait. Since its founding in October 1949, the PRC has never extended its effective control and actual jurisdiction over Taiwan for a single day, despite its militant rhetoric that "Taiwan is an indivisible part of China."

Judged by the international legal requirements of statehood, Taiwan is a sovereign, independent state in every sense of the word. It has control over its people, a defined territory, and a government capable of both governing effectively and acting responsibly in external relations. What is increasingly at issue for the people of Taiwan is whether to call this independent island state of Taiwan the "Republic of China," the "Republic of China on Taiwan," the "Republic of Taiwan," or simply "Taiwan." Independence has been a fact. "Autonomy" will not be acceptable to the Taiwanese people. There is no need for Taiwan to declare independence now.

The nation of Taiwan has undergone a profound political transformation in the direction of democracy, human rights, and Taiwanization, along with impressive economic development. This is what the Taiwan experience is all about.

In the continuing process of nation-building and democratization, the people of Taiwan are seeking to enhance their participation in international affairs through membership for Taiwan in the United Nations and in other international governmental organizations.

With this background in mind, let me highlight quickly implications for U.S. policy toward Taiwan, China, and Hong Kong. I find it helpful to make this summary by referring to the three basic U.S. foreign policy goals identified by Ramon Myers in his introductory remarks: (1) peace, (2) prosperity, and (3) democracy and human rights.

First, regarding the pursuit of peace in East Asia, it is imperative, as Ambassador Lilley suggested, that the PRC make a "no force pledge." The PRC's refusal to renounce the threat of force in settling disputes with Taiwan has been a continuing source of insecurity, instability, and anxiety in the Taiwan Strait area. The idea of dealing with Taiwan's future in a peaceful way has been the cornerstone of the U.S. "one-China policy," as emphasized in the Taiwan Relations Act of 1979 and in the three joint communiqués between the United States and the PRC. Whenever the United States reaffirms its "one-China–but not now" policy, as Richard Solomon characterized it, the United States should simultaneously reaffirm its policy of seeking a *peaceful* solution. Such a framework of peace and stability would serve the common interests of all parties concerned. A treaty of friendship, commerce, and navigation between Taiwan and China, on the basis of equality and mutual benefits in accord with international law and practice, would also contribute to such a framework of peaceful interaction and competition. Multilateral security arrangements within the larger Pacific community context that embraces both Taiwan and China would be helpful.

Second, Taiwan remains very much in the mainstream of global trade and the free market economy, despite having developed close economic ties with China in recent years. Taiwan is the fourteenth-largest trading state in the world and the fifth-largest trading partner of the United States. Taiwan has been a leading holder of foreign exchange reserves for years. It would not serve Taiwan's best economic interests to be identified as part of the "greater China" trade bloc.

In the same vein, it would serve the best interests of the United States and the world economy at large to facilitate the free flow of goods and services globally, not to contribute—wittingly or unwittingly—to the formation of a greater China trade bloc. Therefore, applications for membership in the General Agreement on Tariffs and Trade

(GATT) by Taiwan and by China should be decided by weighing each case individually and not be treated as a package deal. I agree with Nicholas Lardy that China's demands for concessions in obtaining GATT membership should be carefully considered issue by issue.

Third, a focus on human rights has become a salient feature of contemporary international law and affairs. Human rights, as expressed in the Universal Declaration of Human Rights and the two International Covenants on Human Rights, have become the yardstick by which the legitimacy of a government is judged. Human rights have become a matter of international concern. No country should be immune from international human rights scrutiny.

This emphasis on human rights should continue to be an integral part of U.S. foreign policy, as Merle Goldman suggested. After delinkage of human rights from most favored nation status, the United States should continue a consistent, even-handed human rights policy as part of its overall foreign policy. Whenever there are gross violations of human rights—whoever the violators may be—the United States must speak up. Steadfastness and consistency in the formulation and execution of human rights policy are essential. Quiet diplomacy is no substitute for public condemnation or expressions of disapproval. Taiwan's membership in the United Nations and in other international governmental organizations is a matter of fundamental human rights for Taiwan's 21 million people. It is a matter of *simple justice*. To support Taiwan's membership in the United Nations is the *right* thing to do.

Taiwan can contribute to the United Nations and other international governmental organizations both financially and otherwise. Taiwan, in particular, can share the Taiwan experience with others. The Taiwan experience has two dimensions: the economic dimension and the political dimension in terms of democracy and the protection of human rights.

Those who are genuinely concerned about the future of the Chinese people should take into account the political dimension of the Taiwan experience as well. Promoting democracy and human rights for the Chinese people would serve the long-term interests of China.

A Realistic Policy toward Greater China

HUNGDAH CHIU

On February 6, 1922, the Treaty on Principles and Policies concerning China (Nine-Power Treaty)[1] was signed in Washington, D.C. Article 1 of the treaty provides for a basic policy commitment of the United States, Belgium, the United Kingdom, Canada, Australia, New Zealand, South Africa, India, France, Italy, Japan, the Netherlands, and Portugal toward China as follows:

The Contracting Powers, other than China, agree:

1. To respect the sovereignty, the independence, and the territorial and administrative integrity of China [i.e., the Republic of China];

2. To provide the fullest and most unembarrassed opportunity for China to develop and maintain for herself an effective and stable government;

3. To use their influence for the purpose of effectually establishing and maintaining the principle of equal opportunity for the commerce and industry of all nations throughout the territory of China;

4. To refrain from taking advantage of conditions in China in order to seek special rights or privileges which would abridge the rights of subjects or citizens of friendly States, and from countenancing action inimical to the security of such states.[2]

Although the treaty was concluded more than seventy years ago, it is still in force; none of the contracting parties have withdrawn from the treaty. In the United States, the Taiwan Relations Act of 1979[3] provides in Section 4(c) as follows:

(c) For all purposes, including actions in any court of the United States, the Congress approves the continuation in force of all treaties and other international agreements, including multilateral conventions, entered into by the United States and the governing authorities on Taiwan recognized by the United States as the Republic of China prior to January 1, 1979, and in force between them on December 31, 1979, unless and until terminated in accordance with law.[4]

This treaty is listed in the *Treaties in Force*, published annually by the United States Department of State.[5] However, in view of the United States' establishment of diplomatic relations with the People's Republic of China (PRC), it is noted in the *Treaties in Force* that this treaty is applicable only to Taiwan.[6]

Therefore, any proposed policy change that affects the sovereignty, independence, and administrative integrity of the Republic of China (ROC), which now effectively controls Taiwan and some other islands, is contrary to U.S. treaty obligations. Thus, the United States cannot support the policy of the People's Republic of China (PRC) to annex Taiwan under its "one country, two systems" policy of making the Republic of China on Taiwan a Special Administrative Region of the PRC, which is preconditioned on the elimination of the sovereignty, independence, and administrative integrity of the ROC.

With respect to U.S. policy toward China, including both the Chinese mainland and Taiwan, the different U.S. administrations under both the Democratic Party and the Republican Party have repeatedly stated that it is governed by the one-China policy as reflected in the three communiqués (the 1972 Shanghai Communiqué,[7] the 1979 Communiqué on Establishing Diplomatic Relations,[8] and the 1982 Taiwan Arms Sales Communiqué[9]) and the Taiwan Relations Act of 1979.

Assistant Secretary of State Winston Lord explained the merits of this policy at the September 27, 1994, Senate hearing as follows:

> The policy has been essential in maintaining peace, stability, and economic development on both sides of the Taiwan Strait and throughout the region. It has buttressed expansion of bilateral contacts between China and Taiwan, including a broadening of social and economic linkages that have improved standards of living both in Taiwan and in the People's Republic of China. Meanwhile, the United States has maintained mutually beneficial ties with both the PRC and Taiwan.[10]

However, the successful implementation of the U.S. one-China policy is contingent on the cooperation of the ROC government under the leadership of President Lee Teng-hui. President Lee is committed to the one-China policy, reduction of tension in the Taiwan Strait, improvement of Taiwan-mainland relations, and the unification of China under a democratic and free enterprise system. However, his government must be responsive to public opinion in Taiwan. The overwhelming majority of the 21 million Chinese people in Taiwan strongly opposes discrimination against its basic rights to participate in political, economic, and cultural activities, especially its right to participate in international organizations, in the international community.

If under the one-China policy of President Lee's government Taiwan cannot participate in international activities, including appropriate participation in international organizations, more people, out of frustration, may support the advocates of Taiwan independence because they can make a seemingly convincing argument that only when Taiwan becomes an independent country can it break out of its present state of international isolation.

Therefore, the PRC's policy to exclude Taiwan from the United Nations, other international organizations, and international activities in general is, ironically, undercutting the PRC's attempts to achieve its goal of peaceful unification of the Chinese mainland with Taiwan and in fact encouraging Chinese people in Taiwan to seek Taiwan independence rather than the unification of China.

If President Lee's government is voted out of power, the new government in Taiwan may not support the one-China policy and may even seek a plebiscite (a bill on such a plebiscite proposed by the opposition party is now pending in the Legislative Yuan) to declare Taiwan independent. Under that circumstance, the PRC is likely to intervene,[11] thus creating a situation from which the the United States would find it difficult to extricate itself. Peace, stability, and prosperity in East Asia would also be seriously undermined.

In the light of all these considerations, I believe that it is in the best interests of the United States and the PRC to help Taiwan appropriately to participate in international activities, especially in international organizations, under the principle of one China.[12]

Notes

1. 44 Stat. 2113; Charles I. Bevans, compiler, *Treaties and Other International Agreements of the United States of America*, vol. 2 (Lausanne, Switzerland: Imprimaries Reunies, n.d.), p. 375; *League of Nations Treaty Series* (hereafter, *LNTS*), vol. 38 (Washington, D.C.: U.S. Government Printing Office, 1969), p. 278.
2. Bevans, *Treaties*, p. 377; *LNTS*, p. 281.
3. Public Law 86–8, 96th Congress, 93 Stat. 14 and 22 United States Code, 3301–3316.
4. 22 United States Code, 3303.
5. United States Department of State, *Treaties in Force: A List of Treaties and Other International Agreements of the United States in Force on January 1, 1994* (Washington, D.C.: U.S. Government Printing Office, 1994), p. 309.
6. Ibid.
7. *Department of State Bulletin* 66, no. 1708 (March 20, 1972): 435–38.
8. *Department of State Bulletin* 79, no. 2022 (January 1979): 25.
9. *Department of State Bulletin* 82, no. 2067 (October 1982): 20.
10. Statement made at the hearing.
11. In its "White Paper on Taiwan" issued on August 31, 1993, the PRC states that the "Chinese Government . . . opposes . . . one China, one Taiwan" and "any government or act that could lead to 'independence of Taiwan.'" It also states that "any sovereign state is entitled to use any means it deems necessary, including military ones, to uphold its sovereignty and territorial integrity." "'White Paper' on Taiwan, Reunification Issue," *Foreign Broadcast Information Service: China*, September 1, 1993, pp. 47, 48.

    Recently it was reported that the PRC conducted a large-scale military exercise, dubbed Donghai No. 4, on Dongshan Island, across the Taiwan Strait in mid-September 1994. According to Taiwan's intelligence source, the exercise involved more than two hundred military aircraft, forty-plus ships, and at least an army division. See "Military Head Says Troops on 'Alert' for Mainland Exercise," *Foreign Broadcast Information Service: China*, September 6, 1994, p. 58. It is also reported that a large-scale naval exercise was conducted in mid-September 1994 near the Zhoushan Archipelago, almost three hundred miles northwest of Taiwan. The exercise included more than fifty vessels, many aircraft, and Chinese marines. See *Shih-jie jih-pao* (World journal) (New York), September 16, 1994, p. A2.

12. Both the ROC in Taiwan and the PRC are members of the Asian
Development Bank (ADB) and the Asia-Pacific Economic Cooperation
(APEC) organization, and both have observer status with GATT, to
which they are negotiating accession. It is submitted that it is possible
for the United States to support Taiwan's participation in international
organizations within the context of a one-China policy, based on the
model already extant in the ADB, APEC, and GATT.

For instance, the Articles of Agreement of the International
Monetary Fund (*United Nations Treaty Series*, vol. 2, p. 39) may be
amended to open its membership to include a "separate monetary territory possessing full autonomy in the conduct of its external monetary
relations," similar to that of GATT. Article 33 of the General Agreement
on Tariffs and Trade, October 30, 1947, provides:

> A government not party to this Agreement, or a government acting on
> behalf of a *separate customs' territory possessing full autonomy in the
> conduct of its external commercial relations* and of the other matters pro-
> vided for in this Agreement, may accede to this Agreement, on its own
> behalf or on behalf of that territory, on terms to be agreed between such
> government and the Contracting Parties. Decisions of the Contracting
> Parties under this paragraph shall be taken by a two-thirds majority. (Em-
> phasis added.) (Quoted from Louis B. Sohn, *International Organizations
> and Integration* [Dordrecht: Martinus Nijhoff Publishers, 1986], p. 699.)

If Taiwan's admission to the ADB and APEC and its prospective
admission to GATT are not considered by the United States and the PRC
as constituting "two Chinas," there is no reason to regard Taiwan membership status in the IMF under the above proposed formula as inconsis-
tent with the U.S. one-China policy. Similarly, Taiwan should be granted
membership in the Universal Postal Union (UPU), given Taiwan's status
as a separate postal territory; in the International Telecommunication
Union as a separate telecommunications territory; and in other international organizations on a similar basis. Such a process granting Taiwan
membership status in international organizations, however, requires
amending the treaties or agreements establishing those organizations.
This will take some time to work out. As a first step toward resolving
this problem, the United States should consider seeking observer status
for Taiwan in various international organizations under the above-stated
arrangement. This can be done by a resolution of the plenary organ of
each organization. It does not appear that any of the treaties or agreements establishing United Nations specializing agencies (e.g., the UPU)

or its affiliated international organizations have prohibited the granting of observer status to an entity other than a state. This approach may begin with the International Monetary Fund, under which, pursuant to its weighted voting system, the United States alone can cast 18.8 percent of the total votes. (Each member of the IMF is allocated the same basic number of votes [250], but additional votes are allocated in proportion to a country's quota, expressed in special drawing rights [SDR].) Each SDR's value fluctuates on the basis of a basket of five currencies: the U.S. dollar, the deutsche mark, the French franc, the Japanese yen, and the British pound sterling. In the early 1990s, one SDR was approximately equivalent to one U.S. dollar. As of April 1992, there were a total of 951,465 votes, with the largest share, 179,433 votes, allotted to the United States. (See Louis Henkin, Richard Crawford Pugh, Oscar Schachter, and Hans Smit, *International Law: Cases and Materials*, 3d ed. [Saint Paul, Minn.: West Publishing Co. 1993], p. 1422.)

U.S. Policy and Greater China

CHARLES HILL

In the course of this conference several people have mentioned that one or another issue may be of critical importance not only to China and to Asia but to the world. I would like to focus for a moment on the global perspective. Many highly technical political, legal, and economic problems and solutions have been raised here, but I am afraid that we may too often be inclined to use such specialized approaches as a way to avoid facing the clearer yet more difficult choices presented in fundamental policy decision making. When the policy choice is clear, and the option taken is understood and carried out with will and determination, the technical details can usually be formulated to put that policy into effect. So I want briefly to review some of these fundamentals.

When I make a list of the major concepts that have been discussed in the various sessions of this conference, I come up with six:

- THE STATE. Questions about what kind of entity should qualify as a state, what sovereign right it possesses, and what recognition should be given it

- LAW. Specifically international law, in the sense of a common framework for commercial and civil interaction that is constant across countries and cultures

- INTERNATIONAL ORGANIZATIONS. Who should participate in them, what membership means, and what is the proper balance among bilateral and multilateral activities

- TRADE AND DEVELOPMENT. While open trade seems ever more widely supported, serious questions persist about protectionism and managed trade; the striking achievement of development by some countries actually has helped contribute to a collapse of the old development paradigm and a loss of interest on the part of developed countries toward those still unable to transcend their status among the poorest

- HUMAN RIGHTS AND DEMOCRACY. Even as the Vienna World Conference on Human Rights categorically reaffirmed the universal character and of commitment to the basic principles of human rights, questions are raised about their applicability or appropriateness for some cultures as well as about the so-called necessity for them to come further down the line after economic prosperity has been achieved and a middle class has come into existence

- SECURITY. Every region in every era must find its means of maintaining international security. The cold war was such a system but a dangerous and undesirable one. Today the choice is between the old techniques of the balance of power or the renewed possibilities of collective security. Isolationism is not an option.

Looking over this list of the main concepts that have emerged in the course of this conference, it can be seen that these are the same fundamental concepts and principles that comprise what we might call the modern international system of cooperation. There is, of course, no formal international "system." But for three centuries or more, patterns of international cooperation have been building around this set of concepts.

In the twentieth century, very significant progress was made in all these areas. Equally or even more important, these concepts were gravely challenged during the course of this century by two world wars and by the cold war. During the four decades or more of the U.S.-Soviet contest, communist ideology directly confronted and sought to demolish—intellectually and structurally—every single one of these principles. And during that era the so-called Third World largely supported Soviet ideological positions on these matters: the state should wither away; law was a tool of class exploitation; international organizations were instruments of Western hegemony suitable only to be manipulated against the West; free trade was the means of American imperialist expansion, and only socialist development could serve the needs of the poor nations of the world; economic human rights should override political freedom, and democracy was fading away under the pressure of the far more effective concept of "democratic centralism"; and true security could only exist for those in the socialist camp, for all other parts of the world comprised a zone of war and oppression.

When I first came to Hoover in 1989 I found that Stanford undergraduates were still being assigned books, by well-known American professors, that not only took these ideological points seriously but declared that their triumph on a global scale was not far off, in view of America's supposed decline.

From my vantage point today at the United Nations, I would say that the most remarkable transformation that has come with the new decade of the 1990s is that the Third World, or what remains of it, now is deeply committed to the concepts and principles of the international system as they have been built and defended in the modern era by the West and particularly in the 1980s by the United States.

This conference is about the East, centered on China, and the West, centered on the United States; the "rest" of the world today knows where it stands on these big concepts: there is a revised awareness of the importance of the state as the foundation stone of international cooperation. There is a recognition that international law is a protective factor and a key to commercial success. International organizations, governmental and nongovernmental, are proliferating to address the newly felt needs of globalization. Trade—open trade—is supported as never before; development is felt to be in need of a new rationale. Human rights and democracy are recognized not only as ideals but as practical necessities for economic and social progress in an information age that requires communication and creativity. And security is of increasing concern as regional conflicts flare up all over. The United Nations is seen by these nations of "the rest" of the world as an essential factor for international peace and security in the post–cold war period, when the great powers no longer take a universalistic interest in the breakdown of order or the failure of justice in remote areas of the world.

What is the significance of all this for the subject of this conference, "The United States and the Greater China"? To make my point, I'll refer to my own experience. I started out as a "China watcher." I was assigned as political officer to the U.S. Consulate-General in Hong Kong just as the "Great Proletarian Cultural Revolution" was launched by Mao. I worked intensively on the Cultural Revolution for four years and then went to Harvard to teach and write about it. Then, twenty years ago, I made a major career decision that displays my analytic powers: I decided that, with the end of the Cultural Revolution, China would never be as interesting again, so I switched my focus of interest to the Middle East and the Arab-Israeli conflict.

Today, somewhat sheepishly, I find myself on this panel on China. And I am compelled to admit that I was wrong twenty years ago. Today the most interesting and significant issues are being discussed and decided in the context of China, the greater China, and its relations with the world. The East and the West are not the same East and West as in the cold war, but they remain at the heart of the global future.

What is striking, from my point of view, is that the U.S.-China agenda parallels the agenda of concepts that have structured international affairs throughout the modern era. But—and it's a serious but—the traditional defenders of these concepts, the United States and the West, have substantially slackened their resolve. China, on the other hand, as it grows in wealth and power, seems increasingly ready to overlook, ignore, or push aside these concepts, or to employ them when to do so would benefit the PRC's interest and not to employ them when another might benefit.

At this moment in history, when a renewed international order is greatly needed and the possibilities for its success are unusually propitious, it is of considerable concern that neither the PRC nor the United States seems concerned about taking decisions that would foster peace, development, and security on a wider scale and in a durable manner. This focus on the immediate aspects of issues does not further the cause of long-term stability in China, in the region, or in the world. The rise to wealth and power raises the stakes. As the stakes get higher, the differences become sharper and confrontations more likely to occur over questions of conflicting state sovereignties, for example. In this context, when we then look to see how the security structures of the region are placed to absorb, deflect, or resolve such disputes, we see virtually no such security structures in place or effectively available.

Thus, we may be at a moment when the modern international system not only may fail to be consolidated and strengthened. It could well begin to weaken and be abandoned in some of its most significant aspects.

If this is to be the case, a familiar alternative can always be called into use: the balance of power. But this now is a world in which the United States shows no inclination to play the role of constructive balancer and intervener that it had during the cold war. This now is a world in which the powers of Asia could well become the focus of a new pattern of nuclear arms buildup following its own calculus of nuclear deterrence through mutual threat, and these forces could play themselves out against the backdrop of an as-yet unresolved aspect of Asian and world history: the Chinese revolution, which has been going on for at least a century and a half, is not over yet.

All this leads me to one general conclusion regarding the topic of "U.S. Policy and the Greater China." It is that the United States must closely attend to the six concepts set forth here and take their furtherance as the foundation of a policy of greater engagement, purpose, and principle with the full range of issues that are accompanying China's rise to global power.

CONTRIBUTORS

GUO CHANGLIN is the director of the Division of North American Studies at the China Institute of Contemporary International Relations, Beijing, China.

LUNG-CHU CHEN is a professor of law at the New York Law School and research affiliate in law at the Yale Law School. He is also president of the North America Taiwanese Professors' Association.

HUNGDAH CHIU is the director of the East Asian Legal Studies Program at the School of Law, University of Maryland at Baltimore.

MERLE GOLDMAN is a professor of Chinese history at Boston University and the author of the recent book *Sowing the Seeds of Democracy in China*. She was a member of the U.S. delegation to the 1993 U.N. Commission on Human Rights.

CHARLES HILL is a senior research fellow at the Hoover Institution; diplomat in residence at Yale University; and a special consultant on policy to the secretary-general of the United Nations. In 1983–1985, he was chief of staff, Department of State.

DAVID M. LAMPTON is the president of the National Committee on the U.S. and China, New York. His publications include articles in *Foreign Affairs* and *China Quarterly*.

NICHOLAS R. LARDY was the director of the Henry M. Jackson School of International Studies, University of Washington. He currently is a senior fellow at Brookings Institute.

JAMES R. LILLEY is a resident fellow and director of East Asian Studies at the American Enterprise Institute. Formerly, he was U.S. ambassador to the People's Republic of China, U.S. ambassador to the Republic of Korea, assistant secretary of defense for international security affairs, and director of the American Institute in Taiwan.

THOMAS A. METZGER is a senior fellow at the Hoover Institution and professor emeritus of the University of California, San Diego. He has held visiting professorships in Taipei, Hong Kong, and Shanghai.

RAMON H. MYERS is a senior fellow and curator-scholar of the East Asian Collection at the Hoover Institution and the author of various studies on U.S.-Taiwan relations.

INDEX